GOT TO BE *Real*

THERE IS NO FAKING IT WITH GOD

PASTOR WILBERT WATSON

Copyright © 2024 Pastor Wilbert Watson.

All rights reserved. No part of this book may be reproduced, stored, or transmitted by any means—whether auditory, graphic, mechanical, or electronic—without written permission of both publisher and author, except in the case of brief excerpts used in critical articles and reviews. Unauthorized reproduction of any part of this work is illegal and is punishable by law.

ISBN: 979-8-89419-271-0 (sc)
ISBN: 979-8-89419-272-7 (hc)
ISBN: 979-8-89419-273-4 (e)

Because of the dynamic nature of the Internet, any web addresses or links contained in this book may have changed since publication and may no longer be valid. The views expressed in this work are solely those of the author and do not necessarily reflect the views of the publisher, and the publisher hereby disclaims any responsibility for them.

One Galleria Blvd., Suite 1900, Metairie, LA 70001
(504) 702-6708

CONTENTS

Preface v

Chapter 1   The Firstfruits 1

Chapter 2   My Love is Real 7

Chapter 3   Give God Top Priority Over Everything Else 13

Chapter 4   Do What's Right in the Eyes of the Lord 21

Chapter 5   What We Think About Most! 28

Chapter 6   Only Those With God's Spirit Can Understand 34

Chapter 7   A True Christian is Saved 41

Chapter 8   Praise Always on Our Lips! 49

Chapter 9   The Gospel is Powerful 56

Chapter 10 The Defect of Sin 63

Chapter 11 We Are Called to be Different 71

Chapter 12 No Part-Time or Partial Disciples 78

Chapter 13 The Convicting Power of the Holy Spirit 84

Chapter 14 Start Living With Eternity Values 91

Chapter 15 The Good Old Days! 99

Chapter 16 My Real Soul Mate 107

An Afterword 113

About the Author 115

PREFACE

The purpose of this book is to encourage as many people as possible to be real with God; got to be real. There is no faking it with God. Our actions definitely speak louder than words and what's in our hearts. God wants us to be real Christians; he does not want us to be pretenders or fake Christians. Unfortunately, fake Christians can be found in any church. There are believers who are expecting to enter heaven but will be rejected or denied entrance. I pray that this book helps many seek transformation in their life through Jesus Christ and make sure they only put their trust in the Lord.

It's virtually inconceivable to see so many people attending church consistently over five, ten, fifteen, twenty, twenty-five, thirty, or forty years or more and are still not real with God. They have not accepted Jesus Christ, our Lord and Savior. Real (genuine) Christians are new creatures in Christ Jesus. A real Christian is someone who has put his or her faith and trust in God.

You may be pondering or thinking, *What is a real Christian?* A real Christian is a person who has truthfully accepted Jesus Christ as his or her Lord and Savior. This person is considered saved or born again because they have applied the belief or principle in Romans 10:9 (KJV), *"That if thou shalt confess with thy mouth the Lord Jesus, and shalt believe in thine heart that God hath raised him from the dead, thou shalt be saved."*

The fundamental principle that makes a difference between genuine believers and nonbelievers is the Holy Spirit, who abides within us according to Ephesians 1:13 (AKJV): *"In whom ye also trusted, after that ye heard the word of truth, the gospel of your salvation: in whom also after that ye believed, ye were sealed with that holy Spirit of promise."*

Although we see countless Christians who are confused about what it means to be for real, Jesus is not confused at all; he says in Matthew 7:20 (KJV), *"Wherefore by their fruits ye shall know them."* You know you are real if you bear fruit. The fruit you bear will reveal the truth about your true character and truth about your faith because fruit doesn't tell lies. Why? Well, Jesus said in Luke 6:43–44 (KJV):

> *For a good tree bringeth not forth corrupt fruit; neither doth a corrupt tree bring forth good fruit.* For every tree is known by his own fruit. For of thorns men do not gather figs, nor of a bramble bush gather they grapes.

Bearing good fruit for God touches more lives than we can ever imagine. So many people do not attend church because of bad fruit; many may utter words as having good fruit, but their actions and words are not lining up or consistent with God's Word:

> *But the fruit of the Spirit is love, joy, peace, longsuffering, gentleness, goodness, faith, Meekness, temperance: against such there is no law. And they that are Christ's have crucified the flesh with the affections and lusts.* Galatians 5:22–24 (KJV)

I wrote this book truthfully not to judge or condemn anyone but to honestly encourage as many people as possible, worldwide, to be real in their personal relationship with God, encourage them to bear the fruit of the Spirit as recorded in Galatians 5:22–24. I thought deeply about Mother when writing this part of my book; she is definitely real with God but also real with her children, grandchildren, and others (my mother's photo below).

I was really touched by my mother's letter she wrote and can definitely relate to her love and sacrifice. She wrote:

> I came up a hard way, without a mother. My father did what he could and taught me to work hard, live life without being solely dependent on anyone, respect and forgive others, and how to pray and love God, no matter what. Furthermore, love others.
>
> My father made sure that his children attended church on a regular basis and serve God with a sincere heart; I learned this from my father and passed it on to my children to attend church. They were always with me, every Sunday!
>
> I worked really hard in various places (hotels, homes, fields, factories and plants, etc.), and hard times in my life. I did not want my children to work in the cotton fields, tobacco fields, hay fields, or peach orchards, but they did at times. They adopted the habit

when they were small because they were with me most times because I could not leave them at home alone.

They worked in the fields with me most times, but I made sure they continued their school work and finished because I did not want them to be uneducated or not able to read. I thank God they are all educated, preachers and pastors.

Many things in life I thought I was doing something big, but I miss one spot. I grew older and lived a fast life. Growing up, my first mistake was, I got pregnant by a married man. I did not know he was married at the time.

I personally did not want my children to come up like I did in my generation. My children thought I was hard on them, but to me, I was not. I was trying to show them a better life. I took my three children to the cotton fields and tobacco fields with me so I would not leave them home by themselves. I did not want to leave them home by themselves. I did not want them to follow my footsteps such as having babies out of wedlock. I had a hard time, struggling and trying to get it together; showing them a dream of hope, a brighter future.

My oldest son, Wilbert, wanted to quit school in the eleventh grade, but I said, "No way, no way!" I thank God that he intervened. All three of my children finished school and college. They are grown, but I still keep them in prayer. When they got married; I was not responsible for putting them together with their mates or separated them from their mates.

I was illiterate, but God brought me through and brought me out. Now, I can read and write after going to school nineteen years. My children are proud of me.

A lot of mothers turned their back on their children; I suggest they need to turn back around, face-to-face, toward their children, and continue to have hope and pray. God is waiting for us to ask for help! Help! Mothers are living in a new generation every year; when people talk, it does not bother or irritate me because they did it to Jesus Christ.

Children, this is your mother; I am calling you all by your names: Wilbert, Patricia, and Robert; I love all three of you! My prayers that God give you all a long life on this earth, good health and strength; that's my hope and prayer always.

Love,
Your Mother

I thank God for my mother and her real love and her real sacrifice for her children's well-being.

From left to right: Mom, sister, Patricia, brother, Robert, and Wilbert (me).

Chapter 1

THE FIRSTFRUITS

Again the word of the Lord came unto me, saying, "Thus saith the Lord, the God of Israel; Like these good figs, so will I acknowledge them that are carried away captive of Judah, whom I have sent out of this place into the land of the Chaldeans for their good. For I will set mine eyes upon them for good, and I will bring them again to this land: and I will build them, and not pull them down; and I will plant them, and not pluck them up. And I will give them an heart to know me, that I am the Lord: and they shall be my people, and I will be their God: for they shall return unto me with their whole heart."

—Jeremiah 24:4–7 (KJV)

The nation of Israel is referred to as firstfruits which rightfully belong to God. The firstfruits were to be offered by Israel to the Lord as a sacrifice of thanksgiving for his goodness and set apart in holiness. The prophet Jeremiah challenged the people of

Judah to remember God. Jeremiah is known as "the weeping prophet" because he cried tears of sadness, not only because he knew what was about to happen, but because no matter how hard he tried, the people would not listen. Sounds familiar?

Sometimes, it seems like no matter how hard we try as preachers and teachers of God's Word, many people just won't repent or heed God's Word. Why? Pride! Pride will keep you from God's Word. Many arrogant or proud people go through a given day without any thought of reading God's Word. They act as though they have no need for the Bible, and they are sufficient in and of themselves.

However, the person who God is looking for is one with a humble dependency on his Word. I'm keeping it real with you.

God looks favorably to the one who places himself or herself under God's Word daily. Even the simple act of opening the Bible in the morning, before you leave for your daily work or employment, is a humble expression that you need God.

Jeremiah warned the people over and over again to repent from their sins or God would severely or harshly punish them. Do you think they listened to Jeremiah? No, they did not. The people flatout refused to hear the warning of Jeremiah, and in the end, the Jews were taken as slaves to Babylon. In the time of Jeremiah, the people of Judah no longer remembered the days when their grandfathers and grandmothers had worshipped and obeyed God.

Israel was to be like firstfruits to the Lord (Jeremiah 2:3), but the nation was not wholly devoted to God. Judah was an unfaithful wife who had not maintained her "honeymoon" love. The people were a wasted harvest, devoured or consumed by the enemy. They forgot what God did for them and turned to false gods.

It was like exchanging a pure artesian well for a dirty, leaky cistern or container. The people were stubborn animals that hated the yoke and were a degenerate vine that bore no fruit. Their sins were so deep they could not be washed away. They were like wild animals in heat. They lusted after sin and still denied they had sinned. Most of the people were bad and only a remnant (the people who remained) were good because they obeyed God.

God said the good figs represented the exiles from Judah who had been carried away to Babylon. This was a surprising answer because the people of Jerusalem believed that those in captivity had been taken from the Lord. Yet, God promised to watch over the remnant in captivity and bring them back to the land. God also promised to give them a new heart so they would know God. At that time, they would be his people and would return to him with all their hearts.

God also promised to give you a new heart so you can know him. Yes, a new physical heart or organ would be nice, but I am speaking of a spiritual devoted heart and a spiritual mindset. If your way of thinking or attitude are unbecoming or very bad, like the bad basket of figs as so-called Christians, it's time for a change! It's time for you to get the basket of very good figs because what life does to us depends on what life finds in us.

The godly remnant experienced good things from God during the exile, but the ungodly citizens or people were consumed by trouble. The godly (the good) remnant made the best of a bad situation because they trusted the Lord.

You may not be able to control the bad situation, but you can control how you respond to it and to God. The important thing is a heart that knows the Lord and is wholly devoted to God.

Believers today are to be a kind of firstfruit of God's creatures, and they should want to give God the best.

Lip service and pretending just won't do. I know this is tight, but it's right! How patient the Lord is with us. He keeps speaking to us and pleading with us to listen to him. God even expects the leaders of his people to be shepherds who love, guide, and care for them. The shepherds in Judah, at the time, were selfish and disloyal to God's covenant. God wants everyone to know they can make the best of a difficult situation. First, live as normal a life as possible and put up with times of troubles without complaining. Be a blessing to others, not depressing, discouraging, or causing troubles. Peace is so much better. Secondly, learn to be patient. God is always on time. His timing will work out for our good.

God's plans never fail. He knows exactly how long and how much we can bear. Thirdly, trust God; he thinks about you personally and is planning for you. Don't fret! God knows your future; his plans are purposeful (they are fixed), so let God work out his will in your life. Fourthly, it doesn't matter how problematic your situation or condition may be or seem to be. Do not waste your affliction or suffering by resisting God. Finally, learn how to avoid false hopes because such paths lead to a perilous destiny.

False prophets and teachers provide false hopes, but if your heart is open to hear God's subtle messages, the Word of God will tell you exactly what to do.

In conclusion of chapter 1, our best offering should be our firstfruits. God always gives us the best, and he expects the best we have to offer, not leftovers. I realize when most hear or read the word *firstfruits*, they always think of money. Our best offering does not necessarily have to be money; it can also be our time and our hearts.

God wants us to be totally devoted! Give God your best sacrifice; don't give God leftovers. Leftover sacrifice is not acceptable to God; he demands our best from our hearts. So we must give him our best.

If the Bible is not interesting to you, please be encouraged to take a simple test. Test yourself to see if you are truly a born-again Christian. Read 1 Peter 2:1–3 (AKJV):

> *Wherefore laying aside all malice, and all guile, and hypocrisies, and envies, and all evil speakings, as newborn babes, desire the sincere milk of the word, that ye may grow thereby: if so be ye have tasted that the Lord is gracious.*

The Lord is gracious! We are to crave the pure milk of the Word of God so that we can grow spiritually in Christ Jesus. If a person finds God's Word boring, there is a problem. The problem is not God or his Word; the problem is with the reading or the reader. Many confuse difficult with boring. Yes, the Bible is difficult at times to read or understand in some places but that doesn't really make the Bible dry or dull. This is why I encourage many to attend Bible study and Sunday school, not just attend church on Sunday worship service or Saturdays in some churches. This is rewarding. It will spill over into your life, and God will transform you.

NOTES:

Chapter 2

MY LOVE IS REAL

> Let love be without dissimulation. Abhor that
> which is evil; cleave to that which is good.
>
> —Romans 12:9 (AKJV)

In the closing or final chapters (12, 13, 14, and 15) of Romans, the biblical pattern is to relate doctrine (God's Word) and duty, for what you believe must determine how you behave or conduct yourself. Apostle Paul discusses your relationship with the Lord (12:1–2), yourself (12:3), the church (12:4–16), your enemies (12:17–21), government (in chapter 13), and believers who disagree (in chapters 14 and 15). But the primary focus of this chapter is real love—love without hypocrisy or two-facedness.

Love for God and for your neighbor is the highest motive for obedience. Love does what is right and just and seeks the best for others. By nature, we do not have this kind of love; the Lord gives it to us (Romans 5:5 KJV). The Apostle John said, *"And hope maketh not ashamed; because the love of God is shed abroad in our hearts by the Holy Ghost which is given unto us."* Keeping it real with you, we can say that we love God and others, but talk is cheap. If we don't have love for God and our neighbors (others), we clearly don't know God. This is just plain lip service. God wants our heart service (obedience and sacrifice). These people (casual Christians) profess as believers but are casual Christians. But what exactly is a casual Christian, right?

A casual Christian is most likely not saved—but they usually don't know it. A casual Christian is someone who believes in God and who thinks that this is enough to be saved. Someone who misquotes or misrepresents the Bible to justify their own actions or beliefs. Someone who claims that "God did not really mean it when he said don't lie, steal, or don't look with lust, etc."

It can be very hard to spot or recognize casual Christians. They may attend church every time the church doors are open. They may worship exceedingly in their giving, financially, and time offerings. They might even be consistently involved in Bible study, church fundraising, and teaching Sunday school. But they may be busy doing things for God without actually having a real personal relationship with him.

Unfortunately, there are people who attend church every week or several years but have never actually been saved or born again. They attend church out of a sense of obligation or for socialization while lacking a saving relationship with Jesus Christ. Once a person has been genuinely saved, he or she will desire to spend time worshipping God and fellowshipping with other believers at church.

Casual Christians are usually false converts who have asked Jesus into their hearts but have never actually been saved.

That's why they are so casual about their faith—they have no conviction to motivate them. Jesus said:

> *Not everyone that saith unto me, "Lord, Lord," shall enter into the kingdom of heaven; but he that doeth the will of my Father which is in heaven. Many will say to me in that day, "Lord, Lord, have we not prophesied in thy name? and in thy name have cast out devils? and in thy name done many wonderful works?"*

And then will I profess unto them, "I never knew you: depart from me, ye that work iniquity." (Matthew 7:21–23 AKJV)

It's after genuine conversion that a man or woman displays a life transformed by Christ, and it's through his sacrifice alone that they will be welcomed into eternity with him. Why do I tell you about casual Christians? A casual Christian can only become serious about their faith after repenting of and forsaking their sins and accepting Jesus Christ as their Lord and Savior. They fall in the category of Romans 12:9 (AKJV), *"Let love be without dissimulation. Abhor that which is evil; cleave to that which is good."*

Romans 12:9 is also speaking of cooperation (unity, love, teamwork, support). We all are part of the body of Christ with a ministry to fulfill, so we are to do our part lovingly and joyfully. As believers, we are supposed to dedicate ourselves to God. We are all part of God's body. Apostle Paul starts off with "Let love."

He proceeds here to specify the duties of Christians in general, that they may secure the beauty and order of the church.

The first which he specifies is love. This word here evidently refers to benevolence or to goodwill toward all mankind.

In Romans 12:10, Apostle Paul specifies the duty of brotherly love, and there can be no doubt that he here refers to the benevolence (kindness and compassion) which we ought to cherish toward all people. Without hypocrisy, let it be sincere and unfeigned (real). Let it not consist in words or professions only, but let it be manifested in acts of kindness and in deeds of charity. Genuine benevolence is not what merely professes attachment but which is shown or demonstrated by acts of kindness and affection.

Abhor that which is evil. The word *abhor* means to hate, to turn from, to avoid. The word evil here has reference to malice or unkindness, rather than to evil in general. Apostle Paul is exhorting to love or show kindness; and between the direction to love all people and the particular direction about brotherly love, Apostle Paul places this general direction to abhor what is evil. What is evil is malice or unkindness.

Finally, Apostle Paul says, "Cleave to that which is good." Cleave means that Christians should be firmly attached to what is good and not separate or part from it. The good here referred to is particularly what pertains to benevolence to all people and especially to real Christians. It should not be occasional only or irregular, but it should be constant, active, decided.

You are probably now thinking, *How can I know for certain whether my love is real?* How do I know whether my love for God and others is real or not? It's actually not that difficult to pretend to love someone outwardly while inwardly not caring for them at all. Apostle Paul says we can recognize true love by the way we hate evil and cling to good.

Real love requires a deep passion for the truth—knowing it, embracing it, obeying it, and promoting it. Just as God hates evil and loves good, so those who know him will love and hate the same things he does. When Paul urged the young Roman Christians to love without hypocrisy, what was he saying? He was saying to be for real; let your love be genuine. Let your love be REAL! Let your love be sincere from your heart. No pretending; really love, don't fake it!

Originally, the Greek word translated "without hypocrisy" (*anupókritos*) meant "inexperienced in the art of acting." It came to mean someone who, in contrast to an actor, is without hypocrisy, genuine, and sincere. God does not want to populate or crowd heaven with a bunch of empty-headed puppets or foolish well-programmed robots. Both can "act" as they are programmed or controlled by others, but neither can truly love. God desires to be surrounded by people who love what he loves from their hearts.

But how do you know if you truly love others and God as you should? Let me help you! True believers find themselves loving whatever the Scripture says is true and good while hating everything that is false and evil. Philippians 4:8 (AKJV) says, *"Finally, brethren, whatsoever things are true, whatsoever things are honest, whatsoever things are just, whatsoever things are pure, whatsoever things are lovely, whatsoever things are of good report; if there be any virtue, and if there be any praise, think on these things."*

Our love as Christians must be real by God's standards, not man-made standards or wishy-washy practices. It takes real effort to grow in the Christian life and be successful in Christian service. God asks for our wholehearted surrender, no matter what the cost! I want to conclude this chapter by really expressing that you do not choose comfort over the cross.

What causes problems in many churches are people not getting along with each other. Brothers and sisters in Christ Jesus do not always dwell in unity. Apostle Paul suggests that we treat other people the way we would treat members in our own family.

First Timothy verses 4 and 16 says, "Not everybody who asks for help should receive. Charity should begin at home, and church leaders must exercise discernment lest they create more problems than they solve."

Sometimes, trouble comes because we believe reports that cannot be verified or we show partiality or we make decisions before getting the facts. Not every church member has a character as good as his or her reputation, so take care. Prove your real love to God!

Pray to God; tell him that you love him and love his creation. Tell him you appreciate everything you have.

The Bible says that we are to pray without ceasing! Do good things. This will show how much you really love God. Do random or unplanned acts of kindness. Do good things. Jesus said, "If you love me, you will keep my commandments." Tell God you love him by talking to him! The proof of your real love for God is obedience. Your obedience to God and his words is the number one evidence of your love.

NOTES:

Chapter 3

GIVE GOD TOP PRIORITY OVER EVERYTHING ELSE

I cannot stress enough how important it really is to put God first in your life. When you put God first in your life, amazing things happen. God does not want us to place anything or anybody before him. He desires that we worship him and him alone in Spirit and in truth. God must come first in our lives!

God says in his Word:

> *I am the Lord thy God, which have brought thee out of the land of Egypt, out of the house of bondage. Thou shalt have no other gods before me.* (Exodus 20:2–3 AKJV)

> *Whether therefore ye eat, or drink, or whatsoever ye do, do all to the glory of God.* (1 Corinthians 10:31 AKJV)

My divine obligation or assignment in this chapter is to communicate that our true living God is very serious about us not having other gods or a substitute god in our lives. No other gods should be in our lives, only the one true living God. The Bible tells us clearly or unequivocally, despite various people's worship of many different gods, there is only one true living God—the God worshipped by Jews and Christians (e.g., Jeremiah 10:10; John 17:3; 1 Thessalonians 1:9).

Although God often works through his people, he is the only God capable of acting without human involvement, the only God capable of proving his existence. Oh, you should've got your hallelujah shout on right there! There is only one God, no one else. God is three divine persons in one. The Trinity is God the Father, the Son, Jesus Christ, and the Holy Spirit. They are not separate, but they are all in one.

In Exodus 20:3, you will see the word *before*. Well, in the word translated "before" in this verse, it does not have anything to do with time or ranking. It is saying that we are to have no other gods in God's sight. In other words, we are to worship nothing else in our lives but the one true God because God is worthy of our complete and total commitment.

We are to give God top priority over everything else and everybody. First Corinthians 10:31 (AKJV) tells us to *"do it all for the glory of God."* We must glorify God! To glorify God means to give glory to him. The word *glory*, as related to God in the Old Testament, bears with it the idea of greatness of splendor. In the New Testament, the word translated "glory" means "dignity, honor, praise, and worship."

I want to keep it real with you; everyone has priorities, right? We arrange our own schedules, budgets, and relationships according to perceived importance. But are we really putting God first? Putting God first means we give him top priority over everything else and everybody. I want to help everyone to understand the importance of really putting God first in his or her life. Don't allow anything or anyone come between you and God.

Let me say don't let anyone or anything come between you and the Almighty God, be it other religions, personal relationship with people, health, beauty, sports and entertainment, material possessions, food, wealth, jobs, power, position, parties, sex, drugs, and the list of other gods. Let nothing separate you from the love of God. Do your best and never give up. Although you may go through some difficult spots or situations in life, come out of it like Job.

Job experienced a lot of things, but he stayed strong. In these times, you ought to press on and come out of a difficult situation as a conqueror. Blessings are indeed in the pressing; glory to God! God is the principal or foremost important figure in our lives and essential to all we do and think. When we sincerely (for real) choose to put God first, we determine that he is more important than any other person or thing. His Word is more valuable than any other message, and his will is more important or bigger than any other authority.

Putting God first means we keep the greatest commandment: *"Jesus said unto him, Thou shalt love the Lord thy God with all thy heart, and with all thy soul, and with all thy mind"* (Matthew 22:37 KJV). In other words, we are totally invested in our relationship with God. We are sold out to the Lord! Everything we have and everything we are is devoted to God. We hold nothing back; we surrender ourselves to the Lord!

Putting God first means we keep our lives free from idolatry in all its forms. First John 5:21 (KJV) says: *"Little children, keep yourselves from idols. Amen."* An idol is anything that replaces the one true God in our hearts. We must tear from our hearts anything that lessens or diminishes our devotion to reverence or respect of God. Like Gideon, who built an altar to the Lord to replace the idolatrous images, we must dedicate ourselves as "living sacrifices" to God, and in that way, put him first (Romans 12:1).

Putting God first means we strive (not trying) to follow in Jesus's steps (1 Peter 2:21). Trying can become making excuses. If you have a habit of making excuses all the time, I hope this chapter encourages you to control or curb this behavior. Jesus's life was characterized by total submission to the Father's (God) will, service to others, and prayer. Jesus glorified the Father in every detail of his life and accomplished all that he has been sent to do (John 17:4).

Jesus taught us, *"But seek first God's Kingdom and his righteousness; and all these things will be given to you as well"* (Matthew 6:33 WEB). That is, we are to seek the things of God over the things of the world. We are to seek the salvation that is inherent in the kingdom of God, considering that of greater value than all the world's riches combined (see Matthew 13:44–46). The promise associated with the command is that, if we are putting God first, "he will give you everything you need!"

Those who put God first will stand out from the rest of the world. They will obey God's commands (John 14:15), they will take up their cross and follow Jesus (Luke 9:23), and they will not forsake their first love (Revelation 2:4). They give God the firstfruits, not the leftovers. The Christian life is characterized by moment-to-moment selfless service to God that flows from love for him and his people. In all things, the believer trusts, obeys, and loves God above all else.

Putting God first becomes easier when we take to heart the words of Romans 11:36 (WEB): *"For of him, and through him, and to him are all things. To him be the glory for ever! Amen."*

I hope God's Word and this book are helping you to put God first, for real. Putting God first is realizing it's all about God. Everything in your life is to be directed to him. Your every breath is to go back to God. Your every thought is to be for God. Everything is about God! Do all things for his glory!

The phrase "God first" or "just put God first" is usually used by an unbeliever. If you have ever watched an award ceremony, many people say, "God comes first." Sometimes it is blasphemous (vulgar or profane) immediately after saying God first. My point is, many times, it was wickedness that got them that award. God should be number one in your life! Plus praising God and cursing out of the same mouth, what's wrong with this picture?

God does not want us to place anything before him. His desire is we worship him and him alone, in Spirit and in truth. God must come first in our lives!

We put God first in our lives when we seek him because we know he cares! When we go to him for comfort on a hard or troubling day, God will give us strength when we wait upon him (Isaiah 40:31). God is the one we must depend on for hope and reassurance, and we find these things in his living Word, the Bible. God is with us when no one else is; trust me. Placing God first in your life should be your daily goal, the main pursuit in the midst of all your other pursuits or activities.

When God is the top priority (not a priority) in your life, you spend lots of time with him, in his Word and in prayer. God should be at the top of the list; God should be your main priority. Another way to make God top priority in your life, aside from spending lots of time with him, is to discover why God put you here on this earth in the first place. What are his plans for you? And then fulfill those plans.

Now let me answer this question for you, just in case you are thinking: *What happens when we don't put God first?* I want to help you.

Firstly, you short yourself from the filled or greatest level of God's favor. The Bible is very clear that God does not show favoritism. Let me prove it; in Romans 2:9–11 (WEB): *"Oppression, and anguish on every soul of man who does evil, to the Jew first, and also to the Greek. But glory, honor, and peace go to every man who does good, to the Jew first, and also to the Greek. For there is no partiality with God."*

Secondly, you will encounter a heap (that's right) of confusion or chaos in your life. Proverbs 3:5–6 (WEB) teaches us *"trust in Yahweh with all your heart, and don't lean on your own understanding. In all your ways acknowledge him, and he will make your paths straight."*

Proverbs 3:5–6 is my lovely wife's favorite scripture. She loves this scripture because we can trust God, and people (including family and friends) will change on you in a heartbeat or a drop of a dime. So, in all times, include God in everything you do because you can always trust God, and he always knows what lies ahead. Finally, feeling guilty and missing out on the liberty God intends for you to feel when you follow him.

When you are a Christian, you have the Holy Spirit living inside of you. One of the jobs of the Holy Spirit is to convict us when we are not living for Christ (John 16:8). God does not condemn us when we have been saved by Jesus (Romans 8:1).

But God does convict us of sin so we can repent quickly from any sins we commit and continue to be sanctified.

Hence, when you are not putting God first every day (not just on Sunday), you will know this in your heart, and, therefore, you will live with a sense of guilt because you know what you are doing. God will forgive you instantly and remove your guilt anytime you confess and repent, but when you don't repent, the feeling of guilt with remain.

Psalm 32:3–7 (WEB) states:

> *When I kept silence, my bones wasted away through my groaning all day long. For day and night your hand was heavy on me. My strength was sapped in the heat of summer. Selah. I acknowledged my sin to you.*
>
> *I didn't hide my iniquity. I said, I will confess my transgressions to Yahweh, and you forgave the iniquity of my sin. Selah.*
>
> *For this, let everyone who is godly pray to you in a time when you may be found. Surely when the great waters overflow, they shall not reach to him. You are my hiding place. You will preserve me from trouble. You will surround me with songs of deliverance. Selah.*

Not one of us will be perfect on this earth; we will always be completely dependent on God's grace to cover us. But we still have to repent quickly to experience the gift of God's grace. If you want to experience the liberty God wants everyone to have through faith in Jesus Christ, you must live for God every day (not just on Sundays, like many). Not putting God first is like buttoning your coat wrongly or incorrectly. If you get the first button wrong, all the others will be wrong. The good news is, when you get the first button right, all the others will line up too.

As you put God first, everything else in your life will begin to line up as well. It's important that I share with you there are consequences for not putting God first. One of the consequences of not putting God first in your life is you will constantly feel lost and out of place in this world. You will consistently feel like you are missing out on what you were created to do, and you will feel like you are wasting your life. God designed us in a specific way.

The goal of putting God first is not to get something from God like a blessed relationship, more money, or better health.

Rather, putting God first is the main point of our lives; Putting God first is the joy! We are God's children, and he is a loving God who sent his Son to die on the cross for our sins. Putting God first means accepting that he loves us unconditionally. Christians often have difficulty trusting God and seeking him first in all things. We struggle to live a life of grace, to place our hope in him, and to please him.

When God gave the Ten Commandments at Mount Sinai, he thundered these words:

> *I am Yahweh your God, who brought you out of the land of Egypt, out of the house of bondage. You shall have no other gods before me.* (Exodus 20:2–3 WEB)

The Word of God tells us that it is vital to put our priorities in the right order and then carefully cultivate each one with zeal and enthusiasm.

Get excited about getting into the Bible! Make it your goal to have a deep, intimate relationship with God. Let him into every area of your life. If you constantly look to other people for answers and validation, pray about this and ask the Lord to help you stop doing that and instead look to him (view 1 Thessalonians 2:4).

NOTES:

Chapter 4

DO WHAT'S RIGHT IN THE EYES OF THE LORD

When writing this chapter, I thought about Hezekiah in the Bible who was twenty-five years old when he became a king and reigned in Jerusalem twenty-nine years. His mother's name was Abijah. She was the daughter of Zechariah. Second Chronicles 29:1–2 indicates that Hezekiah did what was right in the eyes of the Lord, just as his father David had done.

Why do I share this? What we do with our hearts determines what we do with our lives. We are responsible for cultivating an obedient heart that obeys God and his Word. Now this does not mean we ignore our minds or our common sense, but we are not to lean on them and reject God's Word. We are to put God first; let every part of our body be controlled by God's wisdom. God's Word tells us in Proverbs 15:3 (NKJV), "The eyes of the Lord are in every place, keeping watch on the evil and the good."

God sees our heart; we cannot hide anything from God. What comes out of the mouth begins in the heart. So we are to maintain a joyful heart before the Lord and fill our hearts with his truth. Can you handle the truth? If our lips and actions don't line up with God's

Word, we are simply not serving God wholeheartedly; we are not totally committed to God; we are simply self-centered and living a dangerous life, and we rob ourselves of blessings from the Lord.

If your heart is not devoted to God's purposes, then it will lead you astray. Ask yourself this question today: am I truly living right in the eyes of the Lord? When you look at life through your own eyes, do you only see what you are living at that moment? Do you get so wrapped up or absorbed by the conditions around you that you let the conditions dictate your life?

Truthfully speaking, we let conditions dictate our responses when everything is going our way; we consider ourselves happy. But on the other hand, when things are not going our way, we sometimes become discouraged, unhappy, and depressed. We allow our circumstances to rule the way we feel. We see our problems as bigger than they actually are. All it takes is just one touch from the Lord to change our situation and our life. Glory hallelujah!

In 2 Chronicles 29:1–2, there are some strong words about Hezekiah. He did what was right in God's eyes, just as King David. King David was known as a man after God's own heart.

So his great-great-grandson, Hezekiah, must have been a man after God's heart as well. David was known for serving God wholeheartedly. Hezekiah served God wholeheartedly too! He did what was right in God's eyes.

What about us and our commitment to the Lord? Are we doing what's right in God's eyes? Are we really serving God wholeheartedly? Are we serving God with mere lip service? Are we serving God when it is only about us?

I'm going somewhere with this. Stay with me. I mentioned earlier that Hezekiah became king when he was twenty-five years old, and he reigned or was in power twenty-nine years in Jerusalem. His mother's name was Abijah, the daughter of Zechariah. Even Zechariah did what was right in the eyes of the Lord, according to all that his father,

David, had done. Can you see much influence family has on their children's behavior and conduct in their personal relationship with God? Children can learn and do what's right in the eyes of the Lord because of the examples shown by parents or other family members.

Hezekiah became king when he was twenty-five years old; he came to the throne of Judah at the very end of the kingdom of Israel.

Three years after the start of his reign; the Assyrian armies set siege (or blockade) to Samaria, and three years after, the northern kingdom was conquered. The sad fate or outcome of the northern kingdom was a valuable lesson to Hezekiah. He saw, firsthand, what happened when the people of God rejected their God and his Word and worshipped other gods.

Many people may think they are getting away when they are not doing what's right in God's eyes. What makes it really bad is when we know right from wrong but still do wrong anyway! God is not going to let disobedience go on forever. God will sooner or later get fed up.

So those who desire to continue disobeying God's Word will experience God's consequences for disobedience. Ask yourself, do I push away the truth from my life to do my own thing?

Am I worshipping God and thanking God for all that he has done for me? Is there anything in my life more important to me than my relationship with God? Am I involved in an ungodly relationship?

Hezekiah reigned twenty-nine years in Jerusalem. He was one of the better kings of Judah and had a long and mostly blessed reign. No doubt, his mother was a godly and important influence on his life. His mother was the daughter of Zechariah, most likely the same person mentioned by the prophet Isaiah in Isaiah 8:2 as a "faithful witness." When Hezekiah became king, the situation at the temple was not unlike or different than the condition of some churches today!

Closed doors speak of no access to God and no service for him. God has set before us an open door, but some close it. In the Temple, the lamps were out, which indicates no witness, and the incense altar was cold, which signifies that no prayer was going up to God. There were no sacrifices on the altar, but there was plenty of rubbish (waste) in the temple. No wonder the nation was experiencing the wrath of God instead of the blessing of God.

King Hezekiah's formula for revival was simple: sanctification, sacrifice, and song. He started with the priests and Levites; if God's servants are not clean, God cannot bless their work. If the pastor and preachers of the Gospel are not clean, God cannot bless their work. King Hezekiah started with priests and Levites because if God's servants are not clean, he cannot bless their work. Then, the priests sanctified the temple, offered the sacrifices, and sang the song of the Lord.

We must do what's right in the eyes of the Lord. I cannot assume you love God like I do, but I do know you should love God more than anyone or anything. I do know God is not selective or choosy with his love. God plays no favorites; he loves each one of us equally. God loves us regardless of the color of our skin. Thank you, Lord!

My divine assignment in this chapter is to let you know there is something to be said about serving God wholeheartedly.

In my first book on Amazon.com titled *Live Life with a Heart Deeply Connected to God: The Condition of Our Heart,* you can read and learn a lot about serving God with a genuine heart. When we serve God with our heart and soul, we show that we live a life fully dedicated to God. We are "SOLD OUT" to God!

We don't find serving the Lord as a chore or forced act of obedience. Serving God becomes a joy and pleasure! Why? Because we serve God out of love!

So many people serve God with their lips; they even try to impress him or earn something from him because they really don't love him and/or they are misguided or ill-advised about salvation. They think that, somehow, doing things for God will get his attention and change his mind about them. I want to ensure you know doing things will not get you closer to God. Keeping it real with you, the only thing that gets you close to God is to give your life completely to him and draw near to him through prayer and study of his Word.

The more you seek God with your heart and soul, the closer you will come to God because he will come close to you. One cannot do what's right in the eyes of the Lord unless he or she loves him with all of their heart and soul. If you don't seek God and serve him wholeheartedly, you won't serve him at all because you will eventually grow cold. You will more than likely become offended over Jesus, grow cold in your love for him, and turn away from him.

Jesus spoke of this apostasy himself. Please check your heart today and examine why you serve God in the first place. If it is not out of love for God, you need to reevaluate or reexamine your relationship with God. Do what's right in the eyes of the Lord! The greatest gift of love anyone can ever receive is attention. When you give people your time, you give them your life. When you pay attention to someone and look them in the eye, you are saying, "You matter to me. You are valuable."

There is never a moment, never a second in your life that God is not paying attention to you. He notices you twenty-four hours a day because he loves you; you are valuable to him. But this does not give you or me the license to live or do what's right in the eyes of the Lord. Glory hallelujah!

God tells us in his Word, in Luke 12:6–7, that he never overlooks a single sparrow, and he pays even greater attention to us, down to the last detail, even numbering the hairs on our head. I encourage you and others to honestly reevaluate what you do in the eyes of the Lord. Why? I believe it was President Abraham Lincoln who said it best; you can fool some people sometimes, but you can't fool all the people all the time.

Some people may think they can fool me all the time; trust me, think again. I may not say anything sometimes, but it does not mean I cannot see what's going on. I am truly a man of God and have a strong spirit of discernment; I have to control my tongue and put my flesh under subjection.

Some things are better not said, especially when you follow the lead of the Holy Spirit. What we do not "do right" in the eyes of the Lord is what we really need to be concerned about because God knows exactly where we are and what we do. We cannot fool God, anytime! He knows where we were an hour ago. He knows where we will be tomorrow; God knows where we are right now in our relationship with him.

God is our Creator; he knows our heart, he knows our every thought, he sees each tear that falls from our eyes, he hears us when we call on him. So it's important to know who you are and whose you are:

1. You are more than the choices you've made.
2. You are more than the sum of your past mistakes.
3. You are more than the problems you create.
4. You have been created by God!
5. God can change your heart and lifestyle today.

In closing of this chapter, know that everybody has an opinion, but we need to be concerned about God's opinion of us.

Do what's right in the eyes of the Lord, even though it may not make sense to us sometimes. Doing what's right in the eyes of the Lord should be our desire, not an unpleasant task or assignment. I hope and pray that you and others realize from this chapter and this book that if we are not doing what's right in the eyes of the Lord, our salvation is at stake or in jeopardy. If you feel that you don't know who you are in Christ Jesus and what has been done for you, know that God looks at your heart. God's Word nourishes your heart and cleanses your life. If your heart is broken, it can be healed. Your life can be changed! What your future holds for you depends on your heart and relationship with the Lord.

NOTES:

Chapter 5

WHAT WE THINK ABOUT MOST!

> You will keep whoever's mind is steadfast in
> perfect peace, because he trusts in you.
>
> —Isaiah 26:3 (WEB)

What we think about most; what comes into our minds when we think about God? What you think about God changes everything. The Holy Spirit and God's Word are available to help us, but each person must decide for himself/herself what he/she will think and will imagine. Being created in God's image requires that we be responsible for our thoughts.

There are numerous instances or occurrences in the Bible where people showed some measure of spontaneous devotion to God, but when God said something or did something they did not like, their devotion evaporated or disappeared, which means what they said was love for God was not really love for the true living God. It was only a love for their imagined God (their picture of God).

When the real God does something out of step with their expectations, their love is gone. Now that love was not really love for God. Is your mind stayed on God or is it starved?

Starvation of the mind, caused by neglect, is one of the primary sources of exhaustion and weakness in a servant's life.

Philippians 3:19 (WEB) reads, *"Whose end is destruction, whose god is the belly, and whose glory is in their shame, who think about earthly things."*

God's Word tells us, *"For the mind set on the flesh is death, but the mind set on the Spirit is life and peace, Therefore, prepare your minds for action, keep sober in spirit, fix your hope completely on the grace to be brought to you at the revelation of Jesus Christ"* (Romans 8:6–8 WEB).

Our mind loves to dwell on everything but God and remain there; when our mind dwells on something besides the Lord for a long period of time, we can become weary or simply worn out. In order for your mind to be stayed on God, your mind must be renewed. A renewed mind helps us to recognize our true identities in Christ. Set your mind on the things above, not on things on the earth.

You simply cannot receive God's deliverance in your life if you do not renew your mind. It is a basic foundational principle to live the more than abundant life promised in the gospel of John. God's Word says in Romans 12:2 (AKJV), *"And be not conformed to this world: but be ye transformed by the renewing of your mind, that ye may prove what is that good, and acceptable, and perfect, will of God."*

Why? Because our minds are not by nature God-worshipping minds. Our minds are by nature self-worshipping minds; that's the spirit of our minds. When we are led or influenced by the Holy Spirit, we definitely have the mind of God. Satan will attack our minds, and with his attacks, our eyes and ears are included because it is through the eyes and ears that input is given to the mind. We have to guard our minds. In order to guard our minds, we must recognize ungodly thoughts and ideas by testing them against God's Word.

David said this in Psalm 19:7 (AKJV), *"The law of the Lord is perfect, converting the soul: the testimony of the Lord is sure, making wise the simple."*

King Solomon wisely wrote about mankind that "as he thinks in his heart, so is he" (Proverbs 23:7a). In other words, "what we think, we are!" What we think about the most is what we are the most, not what others think. This means we can control, to some extent, what our attitudes will be. We can live in a state of contentment or choose to be discontented or unhappy. We live in a world that breeds or creates discontentment or unhappiness.

The Apostle Paul says in Philippians 4:11–13 (WEB):

> *Not that I speak because of lack, for I have learned in whatever state I am, to be content in it. I know how to be humbled, and I also know how to abound. In everything and in all things I have learned the secret both to be filled and to be hungry, both to abound and to be in need. I can do all things through Christ, who strengthens me.*

The Apostle Paul says that he has learned to be content (happy). Contentment does not come naturally to the sinful human heart. We need God's grace to strengthen us and to change our hearts. But we also have the responsibility to learn contentment (happiness). It requires effort! God does not force us to have a certain attitude, but we are responsible for what we think and how we act. It requires effort!

The Bible speaks of the ungodly as those who are separated from God. Ungodliness is the condition of being polluted or contaminated with sin. To be ungodly is to act in a way that's contrary or opposing to the nature of God, to actively oppose God in disobedience, or to have an irreverence or disrespect for God. Ignoring God is a terrible thing. When we ignore God's rules and live any way we want to, we end up only hurting ourselves.

Some of the Bible's most sobering words are found in the Old Testament book of Proverbs: *"There is a way that seems right to a man (or woman), but in the end it leads to death"* (Proverbs 16:25 WEB).

Our mindset on God is important; allow God to renew your mind and heal it through constant or frequent reading and study of Scripture, through the company of others who obey God's Word, and through a continual yielding or surrendering to the direction and conviction of the Holy Spirit. Jesus's mindset was to submit himself to do only what was the will of the Father (God), even unto death on the cross. Jesus lived a life completely dependent upon the Father, trusting the Father. This is the will of God for us to learn to completely trust and obey him in all things.

Jesus Christ did not let the distraction of his accusers or challenges move his mind off of the Word of God. He searched the Scripture in his mind and asked God for the proper response. Our mind is the most important part of our body. Every other organ can be replaced, even the heart, but when our mind does not function, we will die.

The mind is important in the spiritual realm as well. The Christian mind is spoken of in several different ways in the New Testament: (1) the Christian mind is renewed—we have been transformed; (2) the Christian mind is to be a pure mind—the Bible urges us to live a pure (righteous) way of life; (3) the Christian mind should be a humble mind—this is having the mind of Christ Jesus; (4) the Christian mind is a ready mind—a ready mind, one eager to accept God's truth; and (5) the Christian mind is a convinced mind—a mind that is fully committed.

Sinful thoughts are often something we believers struggle with. Sometimes we have no control as to what thoughts enter our minds; however, we are able to take control of these thoughts. God's Word helps us to recognize our thoughts for what they really are and how to act (or not to act) upon them. Do not copy the behavior and customs of this world, but let God transform you into a new person by changing the way you think. Then you will learn to know God's will for you, which is good and pleasing and perfect (Romans 12:2).

Jesus challenged people to change their thinking because regardless how many times you read through the Bible, if your mind does not change, you will simply impose your personal biases and labels on the words you read. Jesus taught people how to keep their mind stayed on him. Isaiah 26:3 (KJV) says, *"Thou wilt keep him in perfect peace, whose mind is stayed on thee: because he trusteth in thee."*

Essentially, your mental state depends on what you think about. Keep your mind fixed on the Word of God, the mind of God, the convictions of God, the character of God, and the skills of God.

No one else can know our thoughts unless we communicate or tell them. We tend to imagine that anything we think is safe as long as it stays in our minds. But there is one Person who always knows what we are thinking, and that's God. He knows everything about us, and he also knows our thoughts. God knows our thoughts no matter who or where we are. Scriptures emphasize that our thoughts are of great concern to God. He has the ability to read our minds and to discern or understand our motives.

I cannot emphasize enough: stay connected to God by praying, talk directly to God, and listen to him. Instead of relying on anyone else to tell you what God wants for your life, start a direct conversation with him; tell him what's on your mind; tell God your concerns. Ask for what you need and even what you want. *"And all things, whatsoever ye shall ask in prayer, believing, ye shall receive"* (Matthew 21:22 KJV).

God wants his Word to comfort us in hard times and encourage our faith when we feel despair. Satan's goal is to make us feel weak, useless, and ultimately, to destroy us. Fight his attacks at your mind, body, and soul with the truths of Scripture. You have a loving God who can and will go before you. When you ask God for something, don't doubt him. God gave us the Bible as a testimony of his works in the past so we will have a reason to trust him in the present.

"But let him ask in faith, nothing wavering. For he that wavereth" (James 1:6 KJV).

NOTES:

Chapter 6

ONLY THOSE WITH GOD'S SPIRIT CAN UNDERSTAND

Only those with God's Spirit can understand; whoever does not have the Spirit cannot receive the gifts that come from God's Spirit. Such a person really does not understand them (the gifts from God's Spirit), and they (the gifts from God's Spirit) seem to be nonsense because their value can be judged only on a spiritual basis. Anyone who does not have God's Spirit thinks these blessings are foolish.

First Corinthians 2:9 (WEB) says, *"But as it is written, Things which an eye didn't see, and an ear didn't hear, which didn't enter into the heart of man, these God has prepared for those who love him."*

This scripture verifies that a person who is not spiritual doesn't accept the teachings of God's Spirit because they think the gifts from God's Spirit are foolish or nonsense. They cannot understand them because a person must be spiritual to evaluate (value) them.

There are many who confesses or proclaim they have God's Spirit, but they don't. They are lacking in knowledge in the written Word of God, in the area regarding spiritual things, and they also can be easily fooled by a lying spirit. Only the truth can confront and overcome the lying spirit. *"You will know the truth, and the truth will make you free"* (John 8:32 WEB).

Romans 8:9 makes it very clear that if you have been born again, you have the Holy Spirit dwelling (living) in you. If you don't have the Spirit, you do not belong to Christ. But this does not mean that we should not ask for a deeper experience of the Spirit's presence and power. It's important that I inform you, with emphasis, don't believe everyone who claims to have the Spirit of God. Test them all to find out if they really do come from God.

Many false prophets have already gone out into the world. Keeping it real with you, if anyone does not have the Spirit of Christ, he or she does not belong to him. You can see for yourself in Romans 8:9 (KJV), *"But ye (You) are not in the flesh, but in the Spirit, if so be that the Spirit of God dwell in you. Now if any man have not the Spirit of Christ, he is none of his."*

It's also very important to understand you cannot obey God without the Holy Spirit. There are really people who are going through all the motions of Christianity, and they are offering an abomination (disgrace) to God because they are trying to live the Christian life without the Christian Spirit (the Holy Spirit). You cannot keep the Sabbath without the Holy Spirit. Sabbath-keeping shows an attitude of simple obedience. It is a test of our attitude, revealing whether we really want to obey and depend upon God and receive his Holy Spirit.

The purpose of the Sabbath is to rest from physical labor and to worship God. He had a lot to say about the Sabbath in the Bible, and I don't think God wastes words. If we take the Bible seriously, we can't deny that the Sabbath is important. God said, "Do it because I did it. Do it because it's a sign of the covenant between you and me. Do it because you were a slave, and those who work for you deserve a day off too. Do it because it honors me. Do it because it's my day, and I want you to."

First Corinthians 2:9 will lead us all in the way of wisdom and beware of worldly wisdom. Receiving wise counsel is an important part of being in the Christian community. But the apostle Paul expressed that man's wisdom and God's wisdom are not the same. Sometimes people speak for themselves and not for God. Thankfully, the Holy Spirit intercedes on our behalf. Whenever we need wisdom, we can come boldly before God's throne, knowing that no one has seen our fate or our destiny but God. And that is more than enough!

In the Bible, we are told that what our eyes see affects our entire being:

> *The light of the body is the eye: if therefore thine eye be single, thy whole body shall be full of light. But if thine eye be evil, thy whole body shall be full of darkness. If therefore the light that is in thee be darkness, how great is that darkness.* (Matthew 6:22–23 KJV)

Our eyes reflect our focus, and in Matthew 6:22–23, you will see that our focus should be to have our whole body full of light. The primary meaning of "eyes have seen what God has planned for those who love him" points to the mystery of the Gospel, which is not understood by natural means. The human mind cannot comprehend or understand it because God's Spirit, alone, reveals it. First Corinthians 2:6–16 describes the difference between human wisdom and God's wisdom. Human wisdom is limited to what can be observed and worked out with human reason.

Scripture points out the value of reason and knowledge (in Colossians 2:8 and 2 Timothy 2:15) while demonstrating a difference between what man's mind can achieve and what God's Spirit can reveal. God's wisdom, including his plan to offer salvation through Christ's crucifixion, must be received and believed spiritually through God's Holy Spirit. Without the help of the Holy Spirit, people cannot believe what is spiritual, so they reject all spiritual truth as foolishness or nonsense. Christians (true believers), though, we have access to the mind of Christ because of God's Holy Spirit is with us.

When the apostle Paul first came to Corinth, he did not present the Gospel to them with lofty speech and impressive arguments. He presented the truth as simply as he could so their faith would be based on God's power and not human wisdom. "Only those with God's Spirit can understand" the truths revealed or shown by God, including Christ crucified for human sinfulness. Those without God's Spirit are limited to what can be observed and worked out with human reason.

God's Spirit makes it possible for us to understand and believe spiritual things. Human wisdom cannot bring us to the understanding that the Creator, God, loves his people or that he has prepared the glories of eternity to share with them. At best, we can understand this by the intellect. But we cannot trust in it without faith in God (James 2:19). We must believe by faith!

We cannot see God (John 1:18); however, we have faith in him that provides assurance. Faith is necessary to please God. Hebrews 11:6 (WEB) reads: *"Without faith it is impossible to be well pleasing to him, for he who comes to God must believe that he exists, and that he is a rewarder of those who seek him."*

Faith is the noun form, and believe is the verb form of the same Greek word. This makes believing the action side of faith, but you cannot act in faith until you have faith. Faith is the ability to believe, but that ability must be acted upon for it to work. Believing is the action of faith; just having faith is not enough. James tells us that faith without works is dead. For example: you can't have strength without a muscle, and you can't drive without a car. You can have a muscle and not lift a weight, and you can have a car and not drive it, but having them gives you the choice of using them. If you did not have them, you would have no choice.

Also, without having faith in the heart, we are not able to choose to believe. Believing is only an option once you have faith in the heart, and faith only comes by hearing from God. Many times, we try to believe before we have faith. We may even fool ourselves into thinking we have faith and that we are believing. This is called "condition mental assent." It means that we are only mentally "assenting" or agreeing to the promise of God and not fully believing it in the heart. Faith is of the heart, and faith comes from God.

The Bible says that faith comes from God (Romans 10:17). It comes when the word on a certain subject comes alive in our hearts. Now if it comes, then there must be a time before it comes. What do I mean? Okay, let me help you. One moment, one does not have faith, and the next moment, they do have faith. You either have faith or you don't; it's that simple.

When one has received faith, James 2:22 says they must act on that faith by believing. If not, it will become nonproductive (useless) because believing requires faith, and faith requires the action of believing. We often hear the phrase, "The best is yet to come" as if it's a truth that comes from the Bible. However, we should know two things: it's not a Bible verse and, yes, God's best is yet to come, but only if we love God, and we are in Christ Jesus. This may sound kind of harsh or disturbing, but it's true!

Are you really in Christ Jesus? Are you in love with God? The best is yet to come, but unlike the phrase that says, "All good things come to those who wait," regardless of the condition of the heart, the Bible says that "all things work together for good" only "to those who love God, to those who are called according to his purpose" (Romans 8:28).

First Corinthians 2:9–10 (AKJV) says, "But as it is written, Eye hath not seen, nor ear heard, neither have entered into the heart of man, the things which God hath prepared for them that love him. But God hath revealed them unto us by his Spirit: for the Spirit searcheth all things, yea, the deep things of God."

Our natural abilities or faculties cannot grasp or comprehend the greatness of what lies ahead for true believers. Our eye sees natural objects, and our natural mind takes in or captures their colors, shapes, and dimensions; our ear hears natural sounds and can discriminate between what is pleasant and painful, or by means of language, gather the widest, fullest information upon all mere intellectual subjects.

Our heart conceives natural things, can compare them together, reason from them, or think them out in all the hues or types of fancy and imagination. But none of these natural faculties, whether eye, ear, or heart can ever enter the domain of spiritual things. To see, to hear, to understand, to feel, realize, and enjoy these requires a new eye, a new ear, a new heart in a Word, a new spirit, which springs from being born of God and being blessed with regenerating grace. God has revealed or shown them to us by his Holy Spirit.

NOTES:

Chapter 7

A TRUE CHRISTIAN IS SAVED

And it shall come to pass, that whosoever shall call on the name of the Lord shall be saved.

—Acts 2:21 (KJV)

Many churches today have a high tolerance for chaos and confusion in their services, and they may even see the turmoil or disorder as evidence of the Holy Spirit's work among them. But God's Word is clear: 1 Corinthians 14:33 (WEB) says, *"For God is not a God of confusion, but of peace, as in all the assemblies of the saints."*

God is not the author of confusion; those who do not trust in God and commit their lives to Jesus Christ have no hope for peace. But those who are reconciled to God welcome the Savior into their storms. Only they can hear him say, "Peace, be still!" When we are in a true relationship with Jesus, we know the one who is our peace (Ephesians 2:14).

"Jesus answered him, 'Most certainly, I tell you, unless one is born anew, he can't see God's Kingdom'" (John 3:3 WEB).

God is not the author of confusion. Satan is the author of confusion. He seeks to cause chaos, disorder, death, and destruction. We must always be alert and clearheaded (sober mind). Conflicts and rebellions have their source in Satan, the author of confusion, in both the physical and spiritual worlds.

Physical evils in nature and among mankind are among Satan's works that Jesus came to overcome and destroy. Confusion and mistakes come when we forget the importance of God's Word as our unwavering guide. Again, I want to emphasize Satan is the author of confusion; he seeks to cause chaos, disorder, death, and destruction. Confusion and chaos do not express who God is and is not characteristic of the work of the Holy Spirit in the church.

I want to make this as simple as possible but with emphasis. The Bible says a person becomes a Christian when he places his faith in Jesus Christ. This is known as being saved or born again. One must be born again! The Bible teaches no one can enter the kingdom of heaven unless they are born again.

John 3:7 (WEB) says, *"Marvel not that I said unto thee, Ye must be born again."*

I will always keep it real in accordance with God's Word, not man's words or mere ungodly opinions. Everybody has opinions, but true believers rest in Jesus Christ and him only as their Lord and Savior! I am speaking of genuine (real) believers. Hypocrites don't do this (Romans 10:3); they depend, to some degree, upon their own righteousness.

First Corinthians 2:14 (KJV) says, *"But the natural man receiveth not the things of the Spirit of God: for they are foolishness unto him: neither can he know them, because they are spiritually discerned."*

Our natural minds often struggle with what we cannot see and what is not easy to understand. Without any confusion or chaos, a true

Christian is saved! Let me explain what I mean. Christians know for sure they are saved. True Christians can eliminate their doubts about salvation by placing their complete trust in God. When we as true or genuine believers put our full trust in God, we can feel assured that we are going to heaven. Because a true Christian is filled and grasped or clenched by God's love, God's grace, and God's welcome as his child.

True Christians live out their faith by following Jesus Christ in real life. Simply put, a real or true Christian follows Jesus Christ. There is a lot of confusion and debate among and within "Christian" circles and churches. Professing Christians quote the Bible; they claim to believe the Bible, and yet it is quite a surprise to learn that they disagree or argue regarding what the Bible actually teaches.

Why so much confusion? Because some people say they are Christians because they were born into a "Christian" family or go to church. Others believe they are a Christians in terms of a religious denomination ("I'm Baptist, I'm Catholic, I'm Pentecostal, I'm COGIC, I'm nondenominational, I'm this or I'm that, so I'm a Christian").

Some even claim to be Christians because they have done certain religious acts like pray a prayer, have been baptized, or give to charity. True story: some people thought Adolf Hitler was a Christian because he persecuted the Jews. You've probably heard your own versions of the definitions I just mentioned, concerning why so much confusion. None of those definitions I just mentioned fully explain or describe what it means to be a true (genuine) Christian according to God's Word (the Bible).

Christian literally means "of the party of Christ" or "follower of Christ." Acts 11:26 (KJV) says, *"And when he had found him, he brought him unto Antioch. And it came to pass, that a whole year they assembled themselves with the church, and taught much people. And the disciples were called Christians first in Antioch."*

A disciple is more than a student; a disciple embraces a teacher's ways as their ways. Early believers were called Christians because they believed Jesus's teachings. They accepted Jesus's death and resurrection as the payment for sin, and they emulated (they followed) Jesus in the way they lived. These things are still true today; simply put, a Christian is a true follower of Jesus Christ.

Christians believe the Bible is God's Word and teaches what it means to be a Christian. A Christian is one who follows Jesus and does what he says. Christians don't just accept Jesus's teaching in their heads, they "live it" out in their lives. *Jesus answered and said unto him, "If a man love me, he will keep my words: and my Father will love him, and we will come unto him, and make our abode with him"* (John 14:23 KJV).

James wrote in James 2:14 (WEB), *"What good is it, my brothers, if a man says he has faith, but has no works? Can faith save him?"* But in Ephesians 2:10 (WEB), after Paul explained how we are saved by grace through faith and not by works, he continued, *"For we are his workmanship, created in Christ Jesus for good works, which God prepared before that we would walk in them."*

Please don't be confused or deceived by others' foolishness or foolish ways and thoughts. Plain and simple; being saved is not the same thing as salvation. Saved refers to being rescued from the power of sin and Satan while salvation refers to inheriting or receiving eternal life. Trust me, yes, we may be saved; yet we are still seeking salvation. Salvation is something that you receive from God. Being saved merely or simply indicates that you are at this current moment in time, in right standing with God, worthy to receive salvation with God.

Although these two groupings of words (saved and salvation), within themselves, have similar meanings, there is a difference. Saved can mean to be delivered from or rescued from something, someone or from some place, circumstance or condition. As an example: you may be someone who has been delivered from smoking or drinking (let's say you were a smoker or alcoholic). It can be compared to the difference between you saying that you stopped doing something versus you making the claim you quit doing something. There's a little play on those words, right?

I am honestly really striving to keep a lot of people from going to hell (some listen, and many don't). I must say, you can be saved today and headed straight to hell tomorrow. To have salvation is the completion of the "being saved" process. It is your final destination. It is heaven "with God," and it is the "with God" that is the essential or crucial difference when we speak of heaven. It is the final state of condition where we now obtain immortality, which in turn means that you cannot die again.

And although we say we really want to be up there in heaven with God and Jesus, and see everybody else in heaven, the bottom line is we value the thought of never dying again, never experiencing any more pain, any more sorrow. All of those promises that we would obtain for trusting in Christ and believing God (1 John 2:17; Revelations 7:17, 21:4–7, 22:3).

Contemporary or present-day Christianity wants to blur or distort the line between "saved" and "salvation." By doing so, they can claim that one has eternal life if they simply call upon the name of Jesus. As an example: Acts 2:21 (AKJV) says, *"And it shall come to pass, that whosoever shall call on the name of the Lord shall be saved."* And Romans 10:13 (AKJV) says, *"For whosoever shall call upon the name of the Lord shall be saved."*

Those who call upon the name of Jesus will be rescued (saved) from the power of sin, but that is just the first step in the process of salvation after belief in Jesus. First, we are delivered from Satan's control so that we can choose to repent, then we must work out our salvation with fear and trembling.

Philippians 2:12–13 (AKJV) says, *"Wherefore, my beloved, as ye have always obeyed, not as in my presence only, but now much more in my absence, work out your own salvation with fear and trembling. For it is God which worketh in you both to will and to do of his good pleasure."*

Working out our salvation is a process which involves testing of our faith. Christians are believers in Christ, but please remember, the devil himself believes in Christ, and he surely would not be considered a Christian (James 2:19). So someone might "act" like Christ, but many act holier than thou yet sin.

As children of Christ, we must live a pure life as he did.

The whole point is to have a personal relationship with Jesus Christ and reflect or show the truth of the Gospel for the world to see, therefore being a light unto the world! A Christian is someone who has repented and put their trust/faith in Jesus Christ to save them from their sins, understanding that all have sinned and fallen short of God's standard, the Ten Commandments. Being saved essentially means that one has been "born again" (John 3:3), being made new because of a spiritual transformation that repentance and faith brings.

One must believe that Christ is the Son of God and obey him as Master and Lord. In doing so and repenting from sin and turning to God, one is saved and becomes a Christian. A Christian then lives a life based on the teaching of the Bible as God's Word and ultimate authority, someone whose life is centered entirely upon Jesus Christ's death and resurrection. You can go/come to church every Sunday and think you are pleasing God, but most do not love.

Being saved means that you accept Jesus into your heart as your Lord and Savior. Just because someone is good and lives a good life does not make them a Christian, nor does it mean they are saved. Being saved means you get to go to heaven and be with God. I cannot emphasize it enough you have to accept Jesus Christ into your life to become saved. It all starts with accepting Jesus Christ as your Lord and Savior. Jesus Christ provides a relationship with the Father and eternal life through his death on the cross and resurrection.

Romans 10:9 promises (AKJV) *"that if thou shalt confess with thy mouth the Lord Jesus, and shalt believe in thine heart that God hath raised him from the dead, thou shalt be saved."*

Salvation is the greatest gift that any person can receive. Eternal life refers to your eternal destination. God gives every person the privilege of choosing where they will spend eternity.

If your destination is heaven, you will live for eternity in the presence of God. If your destination is hell, you will live apart from God. God's free gift is what enables you to choose heaven. If a person is truly a Christian, that person is saved.

Again, being a Christian means being a follower of Christ Jesus, and if a person is a follower of Jesus, then they would have to be saved (John 4:6). If you are a Christian, and you are not filled or controlled by the Holy Spirit, you can be. Confess your sins, spend time in the study of the Bible, and ask the Holy Spirit to take complete control of your life.

We should have serious doubts about a person who claims to be a believer yet lives a life that says otherwise. A true Christian who falls back into sin is still saved, but at the same time, a person who lives a life controlled by sin is not truly a Christian. Your response determines your eternal destination—heaven or hell. Faith in Jesus Christ is the key to going to heaven. The Bible is clear that God has provided a way for us to receive eternal life, and that is in his Son, Jesus Christ!

The Bible says, "And the testimony is this, that God has given us eternal life, and this life is in his Son." Know that a true Christian is saved.

NOTES:

Chapter 8

PRAISE ALWAYS ON OUR LIPS!

This chapter is near and dear to my heart, mind, and soul. God loves real praise rather than dead animal offerings. God wants us living human beings, our bodies, our hearts, and our activities as real sacrifices. The sacrifice of praise is the fruit of our lips, giving thanks to God's holy name. I encourage many to open their mouths and speak or shout a word of praise to God; those words are real spiritual sacrifices that are well-pleasing to God because then you are a true (real) worshipper. You will have a new spirit filled with the Spirit of God and able to connect deeply to God's heart.

"*I will bless the Lord at all times: his praise shall continually be in my mouth. My soul shall make her boast in the* LORD: *the humble shall hear thereof, and be glad. O magnify the* LORD *with me, and let us exalt his name together*" (Psalm 34:1–3 KJV).

Praise always on our lips! I will bless the Lord at all times. His praise shall continually be in my mouth. Praising God is the best thing to do first before anything else. Have you ever been in a situation that you felt like you were all alone? Or maybe you have faced a difficult situation in your life, and you did not know what to do. As an example, losing your job or suffering the loss of someone very close to your heart.

Well, consider or think about the good times when you received a raise or promotion on your job. What do you usually do during these moments? Do you praise God? Praising God makes every circumstance of our lives complete, essential, and very worthwhile or meaningful. The *Webster Dictionary* defines the word *praise* as to say good things about, and it is synonymous to words such as *admire, commend, extol, honor, and worship.*

Well, a definition of Christian praise is the joyful thanking and adoring of God, the celebration of his goodness and grace. This simply implies or involves the act of praising is rightfully due to God alone. God is not sharing his praise; Isaiah 42:8 (KJV) says, *"I am the Lord: that is my name: and my glory will I not give to another, neither my praise to graven images."* Praise God!

Praise starts with a right understanding of God based on God's own Word. Praise includes a growing reverence or respect for who God is, which, in turn, imparts true wisdom to us. You can praise God by singing songs and hymns, clapping your hands, even jumping for joy—the list is endless. We can give glory and praise to our God with the use of our physical bodies, with our hearts and minds, and with our deeds.

There are so many ways to praise God; no matter how you praise and worship God, it should result in respect and admiration of God's power, love, and grace for all of us. Being a part of all living creatures, we are to praise God. Praise him, even when we are faced or in the midst of stormy seasons. Instead of letting your circumstances around you dictate the words that come out of your mouth, only let praise be an option.

No matter what, choose to "exalt or praise the Lord at all times," and you will soon notice that praising God instead of cursing him will turn your focus away from you and your problems and on to him. If you want to create the environment to experience heaven on earth, make sure praise is the only thing on your lips. The Bible commands all living creatures to praise the Lord (Psalm 150:6). But lying lips are an abomination and disgraceful to the Lord, but those who act faithfully are his delight (his joy, his pleasure).

Psalm 34 is David's reminder to focus our hearts to praise God in the storm, even when we are in the midst of battle and running for our lives. Praise God first and trust that he will protect those who worship and obey him. David was going through a stormy season in his life. He had learned that Saul intended to kill him, so he fled (he ran away) from the king. He faced dangers on his way, even pretending to be crazy or insane so another king would let him go. Psalm 34:1 (KJV) reads, *"I will bless the LORD at all times: his praise shall continually be in my mouth."*

It's hard to praise God when life is hard, but God wants us to rejoice in him, even when we are afflicted or troubled. Stay in the presence of others who are also full of praise so you can hear their praise and join in. If you surround yourself with those who complain and speak words of despair or gloom and blame, you will fill your heart with those negative feelings. But if you surround yourself with people who speak words of life, praising God, and believing in God's power, then you will fill your heart with God and keep your eyes fixed on him.

Psalm 34:1 (KJV) says, *"I will bless the Lord at all times: his praise shall continually be in my mouth."*

Praising God is an important part of our victory. The Israelites always sent their praise team out first, before any battle because of its powerful effect. God truly does work all things out for your good (Romans 8:28), but there is always that period of time where you begin to wonder what good can come from your current situation, especially in those times or situations. It's important to praise God for what he's going to do.

The Psalms, over and over, remind us to praise God no matter what and at all times! If you have been seeking God for a break through, take some time to add praise to your petitions or requests. I want to share with you some Bible verses on praising God:

1. "Praise ye the Lord. O give thanks unto the Lord; for he is good: for his mercy endureth for ever" (Psalm 106:1 AKJV).
2. "Let everything that has breath and every breath of life praise the Lord" (Psalm 150:6 KJV).
3. "I trust in the Lord. And I praise him! I In God will I praise his word: in the Lord will I praise his word" (Psalm 56:10 KJV).
4. "By him therefore let us offer the sacrifice of praise to God continually, that is, the fruit of our lips giving thanks to his name" (Hebrews 13:15 KJV).
5. "I will bless the Lord at all times: his praise shall continually be in my mouth" (Psalm 34:1 KJV).

It's important that you know that we are to worship God in Spirit and in truth. This necessarily involves loving him with heart, soul, mind, and strength. True worship must be "in spirit," that is, engaging your whole heart. Unless there's a real passion for God, there is no worship in Spirit. At the same time, worship must be "in truth," that is, properly informed.

John 4:23–24 records Jesus saying, "But the hour cometh, and now is, when the true worshippers shall worship the Father in spirit and in truth: for the Father seeketh such to worship him. God is a Spirit: and they that worship him must worship him in spirit and in truth."

I know many equate or compare worship with singing music in church. This is just one aspect of worship (Psalm 100:2). Please understand that worship is in no way limited to songs. It is a full life response to the object or intent of our worship. When we truly worship something, it affects the way we live.

In this life, we have an ability to choose (freedom of choice) to worship, which we will never have again. When God brings final restoration to all things, and we live in perfect communion with him, we will see him and know him fully. In heaven, worship will not be a choice; it will be the natural response of all of creation to the full revelation of God.

Revelation 5:11–14 depicts this image. The greatest thing you can do with your mouth is to worship God, and when you give him praise from your lips, your lips are fulfilling their greatest design and purpose. If you let him, the devil will harass you until the day you leave this earth; but you don't have to allow it. You can put a stop to it now! Praise stills the voice of the enemy and avenger. Praise is so powerful! Glory hallelujah!

When a multitude of armies came up against Jehoshaphat, king of Judah, he proclaimed a fast and sought help from the Lord. The Spirit of God came upon the prophet and told them that they would not need to fight in the battle. Then the Lord led Jehoshaphat to send a team of praise and worshippers out ahead of his army. The Lord has ordained praise to bring a release of his power and glory. I encourage many to stop saying, "When is God going to do something in my life?" Start praising the Lord instead for what he has already done through the cross and resurrection.

In closing, Jesus is alive and well. As you praise him, you are releasing his resurrection power. Put the devil in his proper place: under your feet. Don't listen to his lies; instead, magnify the Lord in your life and circumstance through praise. Psalm 34:1 (KJV), *"I will bless the Lord at all times: his praise shall continually be in my mouth."*

So what about you? Is the Lord's praise ever on your lips? Will you praise the Lord at all times? Do you only choose to praise the Lord when you get what you want? Do you only choose to praise him only when life is going your way? You have the privilege to use praise as a tool to completely shut out the enemy. There is no room for negativity or evil to live or reside when praise is the only thing on your lips. When you praise God, consider it a step of faith to not only look beyond your current circumstances but to thank God for who he is, what he has done, and what he will do.

What father does not want to be shown love based on who he is, instead of what he does? Your heavenly Father is no different, and I believe, as your Father, it's one of God's favorite things that you do. There is no negativity, complaining, or cursing in heaven, so don't let it be an option here. Instead of letting your circumstances around you dictate the words that come out of your mouth, only let praise be an option. No matter what, choose to "exalt or praise the Lord at all times," and you will soon notice that praising God, instead of cursing him, will turn your focus away from you and your problems and on to him.

If you want to create the environment to experience heaven on earth, make sure praise is the only thing on your lips.

All glory to God!

NOTES:

Chapter 9

THE GOSPEL IS POWERFUL

In these days, many folks are reluctant or flat-out unwilling to share their faith. They just don't get it! Some folks just don't get it because their pride precludes or prevents them from surrendering to our Creator, God of the universe. There are so many naysayers and mockers that are lost or intentionally show or express hate toward God. They are their own worst enemy. Unfortunately, some people will never experience life to the full. They are satisfied with the pain and suffering that they see no way out of.

Some people don't want the hope of things getting better and are resolved to a self-inflicted status quo (meaning class, condition, position, or standing); these people don't get it because they refuse to change, and that is why things are the way they are to the so-called or supposed-to-be Christians; do not miss your chance to heed your calling.

Romans 1:16 (WEB) says, "For I am not ashamed of the Good News of Christ, because it is the power of God for salvation for everyone who believes, for the Jew first, and also for the Greek."

And Mark 8:38 (AKJV) says, "Whosoever therefore shall be ashamed of me and of my words in this adulterous and sinful generation;

of him also shall the Son of man be ashamed, when he cometh in the glory of his Father with the holy angels."

Hopefully, this chapter and scriptures will remind you and many others why we should not be ashamed of the Gospel. Because the Gospel is powerful! But what is the Gospel? Even though many say or use this word (*Gospel*), they still do not know what it really means. The word *Gospel* means good news, and it is mentioned over ninety times in the Bible. The Gospel is the good news about Jesus Christ, the story of who he is and what he did!

The essential or crucial elements of the Gospel are the following:

1. All of humankind has sinned.
2. The death of Christ on the cross to pay for those sins.
3. The resurrection of Christ to provide life everlasting for those who follow him.
4. The offer of the free gift of salvation to all.

The real Gospel message is that salvation is by grace through faith (Romans 6:23), not faith and something you do like baptism or faith and speaking in tongues or faith and going to a Oneness church, etc. True salvation is freedom from the requirement of keeping any part of the Mosaic Law to get or maintain salvation. In Romans 1:16, Paul addresses the Gentile believers at Rome and begins by explaining his mission, which was to preach the Gospel to everyone.

Apostle Paul concludes his explanation by saying, "For I am not ashamed of the Gospel, because it is the power of God that brings salvation to everyone who believes: first to the Jew, then to the Gentile." Because in the Gospel, the righteousness of God is revealed, a righteousness that is by faith from first to last, just as it is written: *"For I am not ashamed of the gospel of Christ: for it is the power of God unto salvation to every one that believeth; to the Jew first, and also to the Greek"* (Romans 1:16–17 KJV and Habakkuk 2:4 KJV). Paul's mission was to preach the Gospel to everyone he met. He wasn't just talking about not being socially or publicly embarrassed to share the good news of Jesus Christ or being too shy to talk to people about his faith.

Apostle Paul, the servant of Christ Jesus, who was called and set apart to proclaim the Gospel of God to Jews and Gentiles (non-Jewish) alike: he was not ashamed to take the good news of the lowly carpenter (Jesus Christ) who died for the sin of the world and rose again the third day to the sophisticated capital of the Roman empire. Apostle Paul did not hesitate to proclaim the Gospel of Christ to a skeptical or disbelieving world of fallen men (people). Despite Apostle Paul's message being a stumbling block to the proud Jewish nation and foolishness to educated Greek citizens, he knew that the Gospel of Jesus Christ is "the power of God" unto salvation for everyone who believes (key, for everyone who believes).

First Corinthians 15:33 (KJV) says, *"Be not deceived: evil communications corrupt good manners."*

And 2 Corinthians 6:14 (KJV) says, *"Be ye not unequally yoked together with unbelievers:"*

Being unequally yoked is more dangerous than you think. Paul's warning in 2 Corinthians 6:14 is part of a larger discussion or dialogue to the church at Corinth on the Christian life. He discouraged them from being in an unequal partnership with unbelievers because believers and unbelievers are opposites (contraries), just as light and darkness are opposites. They simply have nothing in common, just as Christ has nothing in common with Belial or worthlessness (2 Corinthians 6:15).

For a Christian to enter into a partnership with an unbeliever is to court or invite disaster. Unbelievers have opposite worldviews and morals; their decisions will reflect the worldview of one partner or the other. For the relationship to work, one or the other must abandon or leave his/her moral center and move toward that of the other. More often than not, it is the believer who finds himself/herself pressured to leave his/her Christian principles behind for the sake of benefits or gains.

As mentioned earlier, the apostle Paul knew that the Gospel of Jesus Christ is "the power of God" unto salvation for everyone who believes. Neither Jew nor Greek have the ability, credential, nor capability to save themselves. God alone has the capacity to save fallen man. God alone has the power to redeem people of sin.

The only vehicle or way through whom God offers salvation to Jew and Gentile alike: is by believing the Gospel of Jesus Christ because there is no other name given among men whereby we must be saved. It is through believing on the Gospel of Christ, which is the death, burial, and resurrection of the Lord Jesus Christ alone that we are saved. Because in him alone is salvation to everyone who believes. The Gospel is to be preached to Jew and Gentile alike: for all have sinned and fallen short of the glory of God. All need the Gospel of Christ, which is the power of God unto salvation to everyone who believes on the Lord, Jesus Christ.

I would be remiss if I didn't explain or write about Mark 8:38 (KJV) which states, *"Whosoever therefore shall be ashamed of me and of my words in this adulterous and sinful generation; of him also shall the Son of man be ashamed, when he cometh in the glory of his Father with the holy angels."*

Essentially, this verse means to reject God and chase after what the world offers (worshipping foreign idols): *"Whosoever shall be ashamed of me."* Our Lord hints here at one of the principal or primary reasons of the disbelief or skepticism of the Jews: they saw nothing in the person of Jesus Christ which corresponded or agreed to the arrogant notions or beliefs they had formed of the Messiah (Jesus Christ). If Jesus Christ had come into the world as a mighty and wealthy or rich man, clothed with earthly glories and honors, he would have had a multitude or mass of supporters or fans. Guess what? Most of them would have been hypocrites.

They would have acted or claimed to be believers but acted in a different manner, like many today. They would have been acting or pretending to be believers, but not so. This is hypocrisy! The Bible calls hypocrisy a sin. There are two forms hypocrisy can take: (1) that of professing belief in something and then acting in a manner contrary to that belief, and (2) that of looking down on others when we ourselves are flawed.

The prophet Isaiah condemned the hypocrisy of his day: *"Wherefore the Lord said, Forasmuch as this people draw near me with their mouth, and with their lips do honour me, but have removed their heart far from me, and their fear toward me is taught by the precept of men"* (Isaiah 29:13 KJV).

Jesus is not teaching against discernment or helping others overcome sin; instead, he is telling us not be so prideful and convinced of our own goodness that we criticize others from a position of self-righteousness. We should do some introspection (self-examination) first and correct our own shortcomings before we go after the "specks" in others (Romans 2:1).

Back to Mark 8:38 (KJV), *"Whosoever therefore shall be ashamed of me and of my words in this adulterous and sinful generation; of him also shall the Son of man be ashamed, when he cometh in the glory of his Father with the holy angels."*

And of my words—this was another subject of offense to the Jews: the doctrine of the cross must be believed; a suffering Messiah must be acknowledged; and poverty and affliction must be borne; and death, perhaps, suffered in consequence of becoming his disciples. In a sense, Jesus Christ and his Word, in the world today, many are ashamed of him; also, shall the Son (Jesus Christ) of man be ashamed.

Jesus said, *"As he refused to acknowledge me before men, so will I refuse to acknowledge him before God and his angels."*

There is terrible consequence or outcome when rejecting Jesus Christ. Jesus Christ is the only Savior; he can either help or disown one eternally because of his or her rejection of him.

In closing, Apostle Paul knew that the Gospel message would offend everyone. But he was not ashamed of it because he knew it, and it alone contains the power of new life. Paul knew the Gospel is powerful! Some may not like this chapter or my book, but it's the truth. The power of the Gospel can change people and their lifestyle.

Not only was Paul unashamed of the Gospel, he was eager. Paul felt the power of the Gospel in his life, and he knew it was the only hope of salvation. So, offensive or not, Paul became eager to get that message to everyone. We, too, as believers in Christ Jesus, should get the message to everyone; don't be ashamed of the Gospel.

The Gospel of Jesus Christ is our heavenly Father's plan for the happiness and salvation of his children (believers).

"For many are called, but few are chosen" (Matthew 22:14 AKJV).

NOTES:

Chapter 10

THE DEFECT OF SIN

The defect of sin; the Merriam-Webster Dictionary defines defect as "a shortcoming, imperfection, or lack." Basically, it is something that is lacking or is not exactly right in someone or something. A sin is when you are willingly and knowingly committing an act of evil.

> *Out of the ground Yahweh God made every tree to grow that is pleasant to the sight, and good for food, including the tree of life in the middle of the garden and the tree of the knowledge of good and evil. Yahweh God commanded the man, saying, "You may freely eat of every tree of the garden; but you shall not eat of the tree of the knowledge of good and evil; for in the day that you eat of it, you will surely die.* (Genesis 2:9, 16–17 WEB)

Adam passed on the defect of sin to all his descendants. It's natural to wonder why people die, especially when we lose someone close to us. The Bible says: *"The sting of death is sin, and the power of sin is the law"* (1 Corinthians 15:56 WEB). *"For the wages of sin is death, but the free gift of God is eternal life in Christ Jesus our Lord"* (Romans 6:23 WEB). But thanks be to God, who gives us the victory through our Lord and Savior, Jesus Christ.

The first humans, Adam and Eve, lost their lives because they sinned against God. Death was the only possible outcome of their rebellion against God, for with him (God) is "the source of life." I said earlier Adam passed on the defect of sin to all his descendants. The Bible says: "Through one man sin entered into the world and death through sin, and thus, death spread to all men because they had all sinned." All people die because they all sin.

According to the Bible, death is not the end of life but the separation of the soul from the body. Scripture clearly speaks of both eternal life with God in heaven and eternal separation from God in hell. Death is the result of sin. Some are still wondering, *Why do we die?* I shared Genesis 2 verses 9, 16, and 17 earlier. In verse 9; in the garden of Eden, Jehovah (God) told Adam: *"Out of the ground Yahweh God made every tree to grow that is pleasant to the sight, and good for food, including the tree of life in the middle of the garden and the tree of the knowledge of good and evil."* That clear command was not difficult to obey, and Jehovah (God) had the right to tell Adam and Eve what is good and what is bad.

By obeying Jehovah (God), they would show him that they respected his authority. They would also show him just how thankful they were for everything he had given them. But how did Satan mislead Adam and Eve? Why is there no excuse for what Adam and Eve did? Adam and Eve chose to disobey Jehovah (God). Satan said to Eve: "Did God really say that you must not eat from every tree of the garden?" Eve's reply is in Genesis 3:1–3 (AKJV):

> *Now the serpent was more subtil than any beast of the field which the Lord God had made. And he said unto the woman, Yea, hath God said, Ye shall not eat of every tree of the garden? And the woman said unto the serpent, We may eat of the fruit of the trees of the garden: but of the fruit of the tree which is in the midst*

of the garden, God hath said, Ye shall not eat of it, neither shall ye touch it, lest ye die.

Then Satan said in Genesis 3:4–6 (AKJV):

And the serpent said unto the woman, Ye shall not surely die: for God doth know that in the day ye eat thereof, then your eyes shall be opened, and ye shall be as gods, knowing good and evil. And when the woman saw that the tree was good for food, and that it was pleasant to the eyes, and a tree to be desired to make one wise, she took of the fruit thereof, and did eat, and gave also unto her husband with her; and he did eat.

Satan wanted Eve to think that she could decide for herself what was good and what was bad. At the same time, he lied about what would happen if she disobeyed. Satan said that Eve wouldn't die, so Eve ate some of the fruit and then gave some to her husband. Adam and Eve knew that Jehovah (God) had told them not to eat the fruit. When they ate it, they chose to disobey a clear and reasonable command from God. By eating, they showed that they did not respect their loving heavenly Father.

There is no excuse for what they did, but why is it so disappointing that Adam and Eve disobeyed Jehovah (God)? How disappointing that our first parents had such disrespect for their Creator? How would you feel if you worked hard to raise a son and a daughter, and then they rebelled against you and did the opposite of what you asked them to do? Wouldn't it break your heart? Yes, it would!

Adam came from the dust, and he returned to the dust. When they (Adam and Eve) disobeyed, they lost the opportunity to live forever. Jehovah (God) had told Adam: "For dust you are and to dust you will return" (Genesis 3:19).

Genesis 3:19 (AJKV) says, *"In the sweat of thy face shalt thou eat bread, till thou return unto the ground; for out of it wast thou taken: for dust thou art, and unto dust shalt thou return."*

This meant that Adam would become dust again, as if he had never been created (Genesis 2:7). After Adam sinned, he died and no longer existed. But that still doesn't answer the question: Why do we die? And that's still a great question! So, if Adam and Eve had obeyed God, they would probably still be alive today. But when they disobeyed God, they sinned, and, eventually, they died.

Sin is like a terrible disease that we have inherited from our first parents (Adam and Eve). All of us are born as sinners, and that is why we die (Romans 5:12). But that is not God's purpose for humans. God never wanted humans to die, and the Bible calls death an "enemy" (1 Corinthians 15:26). A lot of deaths are occurring or taking place, especially during the period of COVID-19, delta variant viruses, and omicron variant. When we will die is not a matter of accident or chance; the Bible makes it clear that our lives are in God's hands. God knows the time of our death, and he has even appointed it.

The Bible says in Job 14:5 (AKJV), *"Seeing his days are determined, the number of his months are with thee, thou hast appointed his bounds that he cannot pass."* God knows how we will die; God's attitude toward physical death is not like ours. Therefore, God has an appointed time of our death. We do not know when this time is, but he wants us to live each day to its fullest because we do not know if today will be our last day upon the earth (Ephesians 5:15–16; James 4:13–15).

The Bible says: *"For the living know that they shall die: but the dead know not anything, neither have they any more a reward; for the memory of them is forgotten"* (Ecclesiastes 9:5 AKJV). When we die, we cease to exist; the dead can't think, act, or feel anything.

God explained what happens when we die when he spoke to the first man, Adam. Because Adam was disobedient, God said to him: "Dust you are and to dust you will return" (Genesis 3:19). Before God created Adam out of dust from the ground, Adam did not exist (Genesis 2:7). Likewise, when Adam died, he returned to dust and ceased to exist. The same thing happens to those who die now. Speaking of both humans and animals, the Bible says: *"For that which befalleth the sons of men befalleth beasts; even one thing befalleth them: as the one dieth, so dieth the other; yea, they have all one breath; so that a man hath no preeminence above a beast: for all is vanity"* (Ecclesiastes 3:19, 20 KJV). But death is not necessarily the end of everything.

The Bible often compares death to sleep in Psalm 13:3, John 11:11–14, and Acts 7:60. A person who is fast asleep is unaware of what is happening around him. Likewise, the dead are not conscious of anything. Yet the Bible teaches that God can awaken the dead as if from sleep and give them life again (Job 14:13–15). For those whom God resurrects (bring back to life), death is not the end of everything.

The defect of sin: sin deprives us of spiritual strength and comfort. Sin will weaken the soul and deprive it of its strength. Sin will darken the soul and deprive it of its comfort and peace. The Bible clearly tells us the effects of sin: all sin that is not repented of ultimately leads to death (Romans 6:23). The Bible presents death as separation: physical death is the separation of the soul from the body, and spiritual death is the separation of the soul from God. Death is the result of sin. *"For the wages of sin is death"* (Romans 6:23a WEB).

The whole world is subject to death because all have sinned. *"Therefore as sin entered into the world through one man, and death through sin; so death passed to all men, because all sinned"* (Romans 5:12 WEB).

In Genesis 2:17, the Lord warned Adam that the penalty for disobedience would be death; "you will surely die." When Adam disobeyed, he experienced immediate spiritual death, which caused him to "hide from Lord God among the trees of the garden" (Genesis 3:8).

Later, Adam experienced physical death (Genesis 5:5). On the cross, Jesus also experienced physical death (Matthew 27:50). The difference is Adam died because he was a sinner, and Jesus, who had never sinned, chose to die as a substitute for sinners (Hebrews 2:9). Jesus then showed his power over death and sin by rising from the dead on the third day (Matthew 28; Revelation 1:18). Because of Christ, death is a defeated foe (adversary or enemy). *"O death, where is thy sting? O grave, where is thy victory?"* (1 Corinthians 15:55; Hosea 13:14).

For the unsaved, death brings to an end the chance to accept God's gracious offer of salvation. *"And as it is appointed unto men once to die, but after this the judgment"* (Hebrews 9:27 KJV). For the saved, death ushers us into the presence of Christ: *"We are confident, I say, and willing rather to be absent from the body, and to be present with the Lord"* (2 Corinthians 5:8 AKJV; Philippians 1:23 AKJV). So real is the promise of the believer's resurrection that the physical death of a Christian is called "sleep" (1 Corinthians 15:51; 1 Thessalonians 5:10).

We look forward to that time when "there shall be no more death" (Revelation 21:4). The Bible tells us in Psalm 139:16 (WEB) that *"your eyes saw my body. In your book they were all written, the days that were ordained for me, when as yet there were none of them."* God knows exactly when, where, and how we will die. God knows absolutely everything about us (Psalm 139:1–6). So does this mean our fate (destiny) is sealed? Does this mean we have absolutely no control over when we will die?

Well, the answer is yes and no, depending on the perspective; the answer is "yes" from God's perspective because God is omniscient; he knows everything and knows exactly when, where, and how we will die. Nothing we can do will change what God already knows will happen.

But the answer is "no" from our perspective because we do have an impact on when, where, and how we die. Obviously, a person who commits suicide causes his/her own death. A person who commits suicide would have lived longer had he/she not committed suicide. Similarly, a person who dies because of a foolish decision (e.g., drug use) "expedites" his own death. A person who dies of lung cancer from smoking would not have died in the same way or at the same time if he had not smoked. A person who dies of a heart attack due to a lifetime of extremely unhealthy eating and little exercise would not have died in the same way or at the same time if he had eaten healthier foods and exercised more.

So our own decisions have an undeniable or definite impact on the manner, timing, and place of our deaths. So how does this chapter impact or affect our lives practically? We are to live each day for God. James 4:13–15 (WEB) teaches us:

> *Come now, you who say, "Today or tomorrow let's go into this city, and spend a year there, trade, and make a profit." Whereas you don't know what your life will be like tomorrow. For what is your life? For you are a vapor that appears for a little time, and then vanishes away. For you ought to say, "If the Lord wills, we will both live, and do this or that.*

Why you do not even know what will happen tomorrow. You are a mist that appears for a little while and then vanishes. Instead, you ought to say, *"If it is the Lord's will, we will live and do this or that."*

In closing, we are to make wise decisions about how we live our lives and how we take care of ourselves. And ultimately, we trust God that he is sovereign and in control of all things. It's important to check our attitudes. So many things can go wrong when we function based on feelings rather than truth. Choose obedience that pleases God. Obedience means to do God's will, God's way, for God's glory.

NOTES:

Chapter 11

WE ARE CALLED TO BE DIFFERENT

> Only let your way of life be worthy of the Good News of Christ, that whether I come and see you or am absent, I may hear of your state, that you stand firm in one spirit, with one soul striving for the faith of the Good News.
>
> —Philippians 1:27 (WEB)

It does not take much for some people to cave into adversity or hard times. As true believers in Christ Jesus, we are to stand firm and above all. We are to keep pressing ourselves to grow spiritually. Philippians 1:27 conveys that we must live as citizens of heaven and conduct ourselves in a manner worthy of the good news about Christ. So it's important to live out the truth we proclaim. We must proclaim the truth that as sinful people, we need God's forgiveness (1 John. 1:6–7). We must proclaim the truth that Jesus is the only Savior (John 14:6).

As we stand against the tide of corrupt messages and corrupt people, we must proclaim the truth, promote the truth, and live the truth. Our attitude and behavior should exhibit or show the need to match our life with our lips, our behavior, and with our testimony. But in doing so, it's going to come with a price when we share Christ; adversity or hard times will come.

As true followers of Jesus Christ, we are to live our lives only in a way that is worthy of the Gospel of Jesus Christ.

Don't worry about your persecutors or haters; just pray that God stops their wicked actions, changes their hearts, and shines the brilliant light of the Gospel on to their paths. Shine the brilliant light of the Gospel on to their paths much like he did Apostle Paul who was one of the most aggressive persecutors in the time of the early church. We all experience times in our lives when we are persecuted by our family members, friends, colleagues, bosses, and others. Even though this persecution may persist or continue for a long time, instead of retaliating or getting even as they expect, take it to the Lord in prayer. Let the Lord fight your battles for you!

We must all face it; we live in a society or culture today where people want us as believers to conform or follow to their wicked or ungodly ways. These people want you to conform to what they want and the way they want to live, but God wants you to know we are called to be different; we are not called to fit in but rather to stand out! Represent the true living God through our actions. It's true that actions speak louder than words.

Taking a stand for God is definitely not a onetime event but a decision to live out daily. It's hard to be a Christian today and stand for God. Almost every aspect of society and the world system is in direct opposition to God and his principles. I encourage you and many others to stand with God no matter what or who may come and go in and out of your lives. Continue standing out from the rest of the world. You are called to be different! Because as true Christ followers, we are called to stand out, not to fit into the mold or pattern of the world.

We are to shift our perspective from the earthly realm to the heavenly one. We live in this world as citizens of another world, the heavenly kingdom. Our conduct should reveal our heavenly citizenship (Philippians 1:27). Stand fast; we are not to stand alone in isolation but together in oneness of spirit and mind, striving together, united for a common goal. Striving together, teamwork like athletes in a contest for the faith God never intended for believers to be alone or like lone rangers.

God's plan is that we should gather together in a church in order to strengthen and encourage each other. Apostle Paul was urging them to strive together not just for the sake of their individual faith, but also on the behalf of the truth of Christianity, their common faith.

The book of Romans was written by the apostle Paul to the Christians in Rome who were predominantly Gentiles. Romans 12:2 (AKJV) says, *"And be not conformed to this world: but be ye transformed by the renewing of your mind, that ye may prove what is that good, and acceptable, and perfect, will of God."*

Apostle Paul writes this because he realizes the condition of the people; Jews and Gentiles alike are sinners, and all are in need of a Savior. Those who truly put God first will stand out from the rest of the world because they are different. They will obey God's commands (John 14:15); they will take up their cross and follow Jesus (Luke 9:23); they will not forsake (leave) their first love (Revelation 2:4); and they give God the firstfruits, not the leftovers (not their scraps).

The Christian life is characterized by moment-to-moment selfless service to God that flows from love for him and his people. In all things, the believer trusts, obeys, and loves God above all else. Putting God first becomes easier when we take to heart the words of Romans 11:36 (AKJV): *"For of him, and through him, and to him, are all things: to whom be glory for ever. Amen."*

It's common to hear a Christian/believer say, "I'm putting God first" or they counsel others to "make sure God has first place in their life." Such expressions are used so often they run the risk of becoming a Christian cliché or saying. But there is nothing corny or cliché about the idea of putting God first; in fact, it's thoroughly or absolutely biblical. You simply do this by making a sacred or holy commitment to placing God first in your life.

Choose to make a permanent or irreversible decision to make your relationship with God your highest priority over everyone and everything else in your life. When you decide to serve God with your whole heart and make him first in your life, your soul will prosper, and your joy and peace will increase. Remember to lean on God more than anything or anybody else and tell him: "God, I want to do this, but I can't do it without you." Make time for God, regardless of your busy day-to-day schedule and tasks; make time for God. Put God first.

Putting God first means serving him with everything we have, in whatever situation we're in. It means allowing his love for us to overflow into the lives of the people around us. It's not easy to focus on the essentials to stick to God's plan and to invest wisely, but we are called to be different!

Romans 12:1–2 (AKJV), *"I beseech you therefore, brethren, by the mercies of God, that ye present your bodies a living sacrifice, holy, acceptable unto God, which is your reasonable service. And be not conformed to this world: but be ye transformed by the renewing of your mind, that ye may prove what is that good, and acceptable, and perfect, will of God."*

The most important aspect of our service to God is the answer to the question: "Does God find what I do acceptable?"

If not, then your worship is vain (useless). Many seem to think that God is pleased with just about anything as long as it's pretty.

It is not so: "If I like it, then so must God" (Proverbs 16:2, 3; Isaiah 55:8, 9). True service and devotion to God involves replacing our wills with his; this is the living sacrifice of this verse.

"And be not conformed to this world" (Romans 12:2a). Nonconformity or rebelliousness to God's Word is definitely not beneficial to us. It is certainly not a good approach to discovering the truth of how God wants us to be by looking at the world. When the world demands that we conform to its always changing standards, we choose instead to live by a higher standard. *"We must obey God rather than men"* (Acts 5:29).

The standards of the world include religious teachings; just because something goes under the name of "religion" does not mean that it is of God. Cults, human religious creeds and practices, and carnal social/political agendas are a part of the world. The Word of Christ tells us not to submit to such that these are merely the commandments of men; "self-made religion" is the term the Bible uses (Colossians 2:20–23).

The teaching of these precepts renders our service of God vain (Matthew 15:9). The popularity or lack thereof of a belief or practice says not one thing about whether it is acceptable unto God. *"But be transformed by the renewing of your mind"* (Romans 12:2b). When a person becomes a Christian, it is time for a change. The Bible has many ways to express this change. It is referred to as *"being born again"* and *"becoming a new creature"* and *"walking in newness of life"* and *"putting on the new self"* and *"being raised up"* (John 3:2–5; 2 Corinthians 5:17; Romans 6:4; Ephesians 4:24, 2:6).

This change involves things which we say and do and are observable, but the source of the change comes from within. It takes place within the heart or mind. When the mind is renewed, then the outward changes occur. But what is it that renews the mind? It is the will of the Lord; it is in the effect the revealed will of the Lord has upon the yielding or surrendering heart; it is in the answer, "Here I am" to God's call issued through the Gospel; it is through the written revelation we can know God's will; and it is the words of the Scriptures through which God has expressed his mind to us. The "natural man" may not accept them, but the one who is spiritual will (1 Corinthians 2:10–16; 2 Thessalonians 2:14, 15).

In closing, it's important to know that we are called to be different. It is up to us to prove what is right! The Scriptures also put it this way: "But examine everything carefully; hold fast (cling on or hang on) that which is good; abstain (give-up or refrain) from every form of evil" (1 Thessalonians 5:21, 23). If you or others you may know are sitting on the fence, it's time to get off of it! We are called to be different, not neutral or straddling the fence.

NOTES:

Chapter 12

NO PART-TIME OR PARTIAL DISCIPLES

No one can serve two masters; for either he will hate the one and love the other, or else he will be loyal to the one and despise the other. You cannot serve God and mammon.

—Matthew 6:24 (AKJV)

No part-time or partial disciples—the Lord's warning that we cannot serve two masters. The Lord says mammon, which refers to wealth, money, or property is a master in opposition to God. No one can serve two masters because a time will come when they make opposing demands. Jesus advises us to invest in our future with him by giving of ourselves: mammon encourages us to collect material objects for present enjoyment.

In Exodus 34:14, the Lord describes himself as a "jealous" God. We cannot serve two masters because as Jesus pointed out in Matthew 6:24, we end up hating one and loving the other. Wherever our treasure is, there will our hearts be (Matthew 6:21). We follow what has captivated our hearts, and Jesus made it clear that we cannot serve two masters. A master is anything that enslaves (dominates) us (Romans 6:16): alcohol, lust, fornication, etc.

But what is fornication (shacking up)? Sexual intercourse between people not married to each other. Hebrews 13:4 (AKJV) says, *"No man can serve two masters: for either he will hate the one, and love the other; or else he will hold to the one, and despise the other. Ye cannot serve God and mammon."*

Fornication, alcohol, lust, and money are all masters of some people. Jesus's call to follow him is a call to abandon all other masters. He called Matthew from the tax collector's booth (Matthew 9:9). Matthew obeyed and walked away from extravagant wealth and dirty deals. Jesus called Peter, James, and John from the fishing docks (Mark 1:16–18). To obey Jesus's call meant they had to leave behind everything they knew, everything they had worked for.

The Lord describes himself as a "jealous God" in Exodus 34:14. This means he guards what is rightfully his. He is righteously jealous for our affections because we were created to know and love him (Colossians 1:16). Many people are confused or misinterpret "God is a jealous God." God is not jealous for his own sake; he needs nothing (Psalm 50:9–10). He is jealous for us because we need him (Mark 12:30; Matthew 22:37).

When we serve another master such as money, we rob ourselves of all we were created to be, and we rob God of his rightful adoration and respect. We cannot serve two masters because, as Jesus pointed out, we end up hating one and loving the other. It's only natural; opposing masters demand different things and lead down different paths. The Lord is headed in one direction, and our flesh and the world are headed in the other. A choice must be made when we follow Christ. We must die to everything else or we won't make it. We will be like some of the seeds in Jesus's parable (Luke 8:5–15); only a portion of those seeds actually bore fruit. Some sprouted at first, but then withered and died; they were not deeply rooted in good soil.

If we attempt to serve two masters; we will have divided loyalties, and when the difficulties of discipleship clash with the lure or trap of fleshly pleasure or desires, the magnetic pull (attraction) of wealth and worldly success will draw us away from Christ (2 Timothy 4:10 AKJV): *"For Demas hath forsaken me, having loved this present world, and is departed unto Thessalonica; Crescens to Galatia, Titus unto Dalmatia."*

The call to godliness goes against our sinful nature. Only with the help of the Holy Spirit can we remain devoted to one Master (John 6:44). We are called to be true disciples of Christ Jesus. The true disciple of Jesus Christ realizes there are forces at work that are trying to deceive or trick them regarding what is most valuable in life and, because they are true disciples, they are able to stand strong in the face of deceptive temptations.

Jesus said in Matthew 28:19 (NKJV), *"Go ye therefore, and teach all nations, baptizing them in the name of the Father, and of the Son, and of the Holy Ghost."*

True disciples are trained and taught by God himself through his Word and by his Spirit. Jesus did not simply say, "Make believers of all nations." He said, "Make disciples." True or real disciples become world changers. The true disciples of Jesus are those who learn from the Lord and follow him. They basically accept the Lord, Jesus Christ, to be the decision maker of their lives.

Becoming Jesus's "true disciple" should be everyone's motto; we all have the freedom of choice. The Lord is not going to force us to become disciples; it's our freedom choice. Unfortunately, many choose not to follow Christ, but it's their choice. I am an ambassador of the Lord and encourage many to be the learner and follower of the Lord. Let the marks highlighted in the Bible by Jesus show in your life and many others. To be a true disciple, one must prioritize Jesus over anything else in his or her life.

As a true believer, you should also pray to the Almighty and abide by his words. Always assemble together and fellowship with the other believers as well as a witness for the Lord Jesus. No one can become a true disciple of our Lord and Savior, Jesus Christ, parttime! There is no part-time spiritual life. There is absolutely, positively no such thing as part-time or partial disciples. It is not possible to be a semi-Christian or part-time Christian because once you truly come to Jesus Christ, God adopts you into his family, and you are his child forever. Think of it this way: when you were born, you became part of a family, and nothing can ever change that part.

Some part-time Christians only attend services two or three times a year (usually Christmas, Mother's Day, or Easter). A parttime Christian attends church part of the time; has half-hearted dedication; has part-time prayer life; controls his or her tongue part of the time; denies faith only, but practices it part of the time; and has a part-time devotion to spirituality. They even assume or think there will be a place in heaven for part-time Christians.

There are a lot of Christians who do not know how to be a Christian; they are part-time Christians; they go to church on Sunday, but Monday, they are back living in the world, doing worldly things. They do not know that it is wrong or else they simply don't care. A full-time Christian knows you cannot defeat a full-time devil by being a part-time Christian. A part-time Christian cannot defeat a full-time devil. The devil is the originator of temptation, going to-and-fro, looking for whom he may devour.

First Peter 5:8 (KJV) says, *"Be sober, be vigilant; because your adversary the devil, as a roaring lion, walketh about, seeking whom he may devour."*

If you are serving God part-time; you have been deceived, lied to, don't know, or simply don't care. Satan is a deceiver (liar); he will attempt to deceive you into believing in him instead of what God says in his Word. If you are believing his lies instead of the truth about God and feel stuck in a place of doubt, you have been deceived or lied to.

Perhaps you or someone cannot seem to escape the feeling of shame and condemnation over your past. The Lord says that you are a new creation in Christ and that all things are new.

If you are having thoughts of condemnation and feeling like you are unloved by God, you are under attack by the devil. Satan is the accuser of the brethren. In the book of Job, it says that the enemy patrols the earth, watching and waiting to find someone to accuse. When someone accuses you of wrongdoing, and you are innocent, it may cause you to doubt, fear, and cower. Those accusations can cause you mental defeat and lead to things like depression. Are you letting false accusations hinder your God-given purpose?

In closing, money has the greatest potential to replace God in your life. More people are sidetracked from serving God by materialism or greediness than anything else. People will say, "After I achieve my financial goals, I'm going to serve God." I want to be as clear as possible; it is not possible to be a semi-Christian or part-time Christian. If someone tells you that you can serve two masters at the same time, trust me, run!

You cannot serve God and money; no one can serve two masters: either you will hate the one and love the other or you will be devoted to the one and despise the other. You cannot serve both God and money; you will serve God or Satan. Whoever makes a practice of sinning is of the devil, for the devil has been sinning from the beginning (1 John 3:6).

"Whosoever abideth in him sinneth not: whosoever sinneth hath not seen him, neither known him" (1 John 3:6 KJV).

One of the greatest ways that Satan can work in a time of decision and discernment is to paralyze us with doubt or disbelief in the Lord.

NOTES:

Chapter 13

THE CONVICTING POWER OF THE HOLY SPIRIT

The convicting power of the Holy Spirit opens our eyes to our sin and opens our hearts to receive his grace (Ephesians 2:8). We praise the Lord for the conviction of sin because without conviction, there could be no salvation. No one is saved apart or separately from the Holy Spirit's convicting and regenerating or renewing work in the heart. When the conviction of the Holy Spirit of unbelief comes, there is a grief sensed or felt inside. It becomes easier to repent, and it becomes easier to just pour your heart before God.

Psalm 62:8 (WEB) says, *"Trust in him at all times, you people. Pour out your heart before him. God is a refuge for us. Selah."*

Do you pour out your heart before God when things get tough in life? God asks us to cast our cares upon him. You may be thinking, *I have tried casting my cares, and nothing ever happens.* Now what? It's a matter of trust; God is asking you to trust him. Trust that he sees the big picture that you cannot. When the Spirit of God comes and convicts you of righteousness, a holy boldness comes strongly upon you. Only through the convicting power of God's Spirit can a spiritually dead man be awakened and beckoned to Christ. To be spiritually dead is to be separated from God.

It was the Holy Spirit's call that touched your soul, awakened you to your sinfulness, and beckoned or directed you to Jesus Christ.

John 16:8–11 (WEB) says:

> *When he has come, he will convict the world about sin, about righteousness, and about judgment; about sin, because they don't believe in me; about righteousness, because I am going to my Father, and you won't see me any more; about judgment, because the prince of this world has been judged.*

In John 16:8, Jesus promised the apostles that the Holy Spirit would "convict the world of sin, and of righteousness, and of judgment." If Jesus promised it, that settles it. The Holy Spirit must be convicting and converting people to Christ today; but how does the holy Spirit do it? Many would say or attest that the Holy Spirit "worked on their hearts" in some mysterious or incomprehensive way to convict and convert them. Some say they had or encountered a bizarre or strange experience as evidence of a "Holy Spirit encounter" and proof of salvation or deliverance. Does the Holy Spirit work on our hearts in mysterious ways to convict and convert us? Is salvation predicated or based upon a feeling or a bizarre event that occurs in our lives?

You may recall or remember in Acts 2:41, 47; three thousand people were convicted, converted, saved, and added to the church on the first Pentecost after the ascension of Jesus Christ. But how did the Spirit convict and convert them? True, the Holy Spirit "fell" on some that day, but who (Acts 2:1–4)?

Surprisingly to some, it was not the three thousand who were converted but the apostles enabling them to preach the "wonderful works of God" in the languages of their audience (Acts 2:7–11). The convicting power of the Holy Spirit is "at work" in the world "because they (the unsaved) do not believe in Christ Jesus." But once a person responds to the Holy Spirit's conviction and turns to faith in Jesus Christ, the other sins the person practiced will be taken care of. It is the sin of unbelief (the refusal to trust in Jesus) that is primary!

Generally, the term *world* in the Bible refers to the evil system controlled by Satan that leads us away from worship of God. The human heart is an idol factory. We can make idols out of anything. I am definitely going to keep it real. Any passionate desire of our hearts that is not put there by God, for his glory, can become an idol. Loving the world is idolatry. We are commanded by God to love the people of the world, but we are to be wary or careful of anything or anybody that competes with God for our highest affections. The world must also be convicted of righteousness; this is something that the Holy Spirit does.

There is a righteous standard we are all held to despite the world's stubborn denial of absolute truth. As an example, being in good standing with the church: the teaching of the New Testament on church discipline implies that church membership involves mutual accountability among the members. This is the will of God for all Christians. The biblical call for a membership of mutual accountability in a local body of believers suggests the need for believers to make a covenant with one another because membership in a local church involves commitment to worship the Lord corporately, edifying brothers and sisters through mutual exhortation or encouragement and service, cooperating in mission, and holding each other accountable to walk in a manner pleasing to the Lord as a witness to the truth of Christ in the world.

As said before, there is a righteous standard we are all held to despite the world's stubborn denial of absolute truth. Jesus promised to send the Holy Spirit: "When (the Spirit) comes, he will convict the world concerning sin and righteousness and judgment." In John 16:8, there's a threefold ministry the Spirit will perform in relation to the unsaved world.

"And when He (Holy Spirit) has come, He will convict the world (unsaved) of sin, and of righteousness, and of judgment."

He (Holy Spirit) will convict the world (unsaved/nonbelievers); that is, he will reprove it or show it to be wrong. The Helper (Holy Spirit), Jesus said, will convict the world "concerning righteousness because I go to my Father (God), and you (apostles) see me no more." Jesus is talking about his righteousness. When Jesus was on earth, he lived a perfectly righteous life. He was without sin! He will convict the world of sin because they (unsaved/nonbelievers) do not believe in him. This is the work of conviction in the Bible: to convict unbelievers of the one sin that they are refusing to BELIEVE.

This world is a sinful place, and without the Holy Spirit convicting a person of their sins, no amount of preaching or pleading will ever draw a person to Christ. John 6:44 says, *"No one can come to Me unless the Father who sent Me draws him."* It is God, through the Holy Spirit, that convicts our hard hearts that we are sinners and draws us to God.

A second action of the Holy Spirit is conviction of righteousness. While the world is busy declaring there is no absolute righteousness, and that righteousness is within our own judgment, David said in Psalm 15:1–3, "O Lord, who may abide in your tent? Who may dwell on your holy hill?" The Lord said, *"He who walks with integrity, and works righteousness, And speaks truth in his heart."*

He does not slander with his tongue nor does evil to his neighbor nor takes up a reproach against his friend (Psalm 15:1–3). For the Lord is righteous, he loves righteousness; the upright will behold his face (Psalm 11:7). The Lord has rewarded me according to my righteousness (Psalm 18:20). Jesus is the standard of righteousness, the model we are to strive toward!

The third part of John 16:8 is the judgment that the Holy Spirit convicts us of, and the truth of the judgment. We are the rulers of our lives, and the Holy Spirit is judging how we are living. And there is a day of judgment scheduled in which justice will be measured or metered out to each person based on their actions and their decisions, decisions to listen to the Holy Spirit and receive the salvation of Jesus or to listen to the God of this world (Satan).

It is the Holy Spirit that convicts us of sin, our need for righteousness, and the judgment that we will have to face to draw us to the Father's love and salvation. It is God, the Holy Spirit, that is convicting you of your need for God, his Word, and his salvation through the shed blood of Jesus. Believers are commanded to "be filled with the Spirit" (Ephesians 5:18), which means they are to yield or surrender themselves to the Spirit's full control.

The Holy Spirit also does work among unbelievers. The Holy Spirit works in the hearts of unbelievers to convict and convince them of their sin and of their need for Jesus. Only two things are needed for a person to move from an unbeliever to a believer: (1) their own sin and (2) the righteousness that God has provided in Jesus Christ. That's what the Holy Spirit does to the unbeliever. The Holy Spirit does not indwell the unbeliever, but the Holy Spirit does make contact with and influence and affect unbelievers. The Holy Spirit does many things in the lives of believers: he is the believers' Helper (John 14:26), and he indwells believers and seals them until the day of redemption. This signifies or indicates that the Holy Spirit's presence in the believer is irreversible (it's permanent). Glory to God!

The Holy Spirit guards and guarantees the salvation of the ones he indwells (Ephesians 1:13, 4:30). The Holy Spirit assists believers in prayer (Jude 1:20) and "intercedes for God's people in accordance with the will of God" (Romans 8:26–27).

The Holy Spirit regenerates and renews the believer (Titus 3:5). At the moment of salvation (deliverance), the Spirit baptizes the believer into the body of Christ (Romans 6:3). True believers receive the new birth by the power of the Spirit (John 3:5–8). The Spirit comforts believers with fellowship and joy as they go through a hostile world (1 Thessalonians 1:6; 2 Corinthians 13:14). The Spirit, in his mighty power, fills believers with "all joy and peace" as they trust the Lord, causing believers to "overflow with hope" (Romans 15:13).

Sanctification is another work of the Holy Spirit in the life of a true believer. The Spirit sets himself against the desires of the flesh and leads the believer into righteousness (Galatians 5:16–18). The works of the flesh become less evident, and the fruit of the Spirit becomes more evident (Galatians 5:19–26). The Holy Spirit has one other important role, and that is to give believers wisdom by which we can understand God.

First Corinthians 2:10–11 (WEB) says:

> *But to us, God revealed them through the Spirit. For the Spirit searches all things, yes, the deep things of God. For who among men knows the things of a man, except the spirit of the man, which is in him? Even so, no one knows the things of God, except God's Spirit.*

In closing, since we have been given the amazing gift of God's Spirit inside ourselves, we can comprehend the thoughts of God as revealed in the Scripture. The Spirit helps us understand this is wisdom from God rather than wisdom from man. No amount of human knowledge can ever replace the Holy Spirit's teaching (1 Corinthians 2:12–13).

NOTES:

Chapter 14

START LIVING WITH ETERNITY VALUES

This chapter is to inform everyone who reads it to make sure they are living with eternity values. Now that's if they planned on enjoying the kingdom of God. If you plan on enjoying the kingdom of God, you must live or start living for those things that please God the most, and it's important to do it with the right attitude. Yes, we need things to live, and God provides these things for us, but acquiring things must not be the main goal of life when we do acquire things.

We are living for things when they capture our hearts, divide our minds, and control our wills; and the result of this is worry. The solution to all of this is to put God first and start living with eternity values.

Matthew 6:33 (WEB) says, *"But seek first God's Kingdom and his righteousness; and all these things will be given to you as well."*

If we have any anger in our hearts, we cannot worship the Lord in Spirit and in truth! So now is a good time to let go any anger you may have so you can worship God in Spirit and truth and with a clean heart.

"For we brought nothing into the world, and we certainly can't carry anything out" (1 Timothy 6:7 WEB).

One thing I like to think about, sometimes, is what it will be like in heaven. What about you? Scripture tells us of so many wonderful things that will be in heaven: (1) a sea as clear as glass, (2) streets made of gold, (3) a tree with twelve different types of fruits all growing on it at the same time, (4) angels worshipping God, (5) other saints and Christians, (6) a beautiful city, and best of all, God himself. Glory hallelujah!

God's Word tells us a lot about heaven, what it will be like, who will be there, and what we will be doing. One thing I never find in the Bible about heaven, though, are people coming there with suitcases full of stuff they just could not bear to part with here on earth. God tells us in his Word in Psalm 49:17 (AKJV): *"For when he dieth he shall carry nothing away: his glory shall not descend after him."*

Only things that last forever will get to go into eternity. I can't bring my bookshelf full of books, my favorite music CDs, or even my Bible with all my notes in it. I came into this world with an eternal soul—a soul that will last forever, and it is the only thing I will bring with me into eternity, whether it is heaven or hell. I want no parts of hell; heaven is definitely my choice. For a Christian bound for heaven, however, there is one thing he may take with him besides his soul: the works he did here on earth. No, Christianity is not a religion of works, but Jesus does say that he rewards Christians for what they did here on earth. Even giving a cup of cold water in his name merits a reward (Mark 9:41).

We don't pretend we are seeking the kingdom of God; we sincerely seek God's kingdom; not play ridiculous, childish, or foolish games. Be diligent or hardworking in seeking God. In other words, be reliable, be dependable, and be steady in doing God's will. Be for real with God, and you will inherit the kingdom of God like he promises in his Word. This is the righteousness of God, which is revealed in the Gospel, and is what gives a right and title to the kingdom of heaven. This is not the righteousness of man but of God and is no other than the righteousness of Christ, so called because he is God who formed or has created it. It is what God approves of, accepts, credits, and which only can justify in his sight and give an abundant entrance into his kingdom and glory.

Heaven is to be sought for in the first place as the perfection of the saints' happiness and Christ's righteousness is to be sought for and laid hold on by faith as the way and means of enjoying that happiness, without which there will be no entering into the kingdom of heaven.

The Lord says in his Word, *"And all these things shall be added unto you."* Free abundance, goodness, and liberality of God; without your thought and care and much less merit; even "all these things" (meat, drink, clothing, or whatsoever worldly nourishment is necessary for you). These things the Lord mentioned are not part of the happiness of saints, only additional to, which means you will have over and above what they are or should be primarily seeking after. Is God first place in your life? Are you hardworking or hardly working to please God? We lay up treasures in heaven when we consider all we have belongs to God, and we use it to magnify his righteousness and advance his kingdom.

It means much more than merely giving offerings to God, although that is important. It means total stewardship of life so that God is in complete control, and our desire is to glorify him. Many people's downfalls are not serving God or pretend they are serving God in public. The real problem is within their hearts. Our attitudes and hearts will cause most to make hell their eternal home. Many think if a person is occupied or busy with the things of God, the true Master, how will this person or persons care for ordinary needs in life, such as food, clothing, and shelter?

Well, the Pharisees in their pursuit of material things had never learned to live by faith. Jesus told them and us not to worry about these things, for life is more important than physical things. For example, the birds are fed because they diligently work to maintain their lives;

they do not store up great amounts of food but continually work. But we, as believers, are far more valuable to God than birds. Therefore, an individual need not be anxious about his existence, for worrying can never add any amount of time, not even a single hour to his life. Rather than being like the pagans who are concerned about physical needs, the Lord's disciples should be concerned about the things of God, his kingdom, and his righteousness; then all these needs will be supplied in God's timing because God has the timing all worked-out, and his plan never fails. He knows how long and how much!

Now let's keep it real concerning our lives.

Nowadays, I see many people playing foolish games with God; they talk a good game; they play unspiritual or worldly games, and they even pretend God is most important, in public; but God knows the real deal in their hearts. Jesus taught his disciples that God's reign in their life and their pursuit of his righteousness was the most important thing.

Some individuals still don't get it or understand the seriousness of DISOBEYING God. Some need to improve their level of truly loving God with all of their hearts and living by godly examples. Believe it or not, when we are not living or showing godly examples, it sticks out like a sore thumb among believers and nonbelievers. Some of us continue putting everything before God, but God has many ways of getting our attention. God wants to be first priority in our lives. How simply can I put it? God wants to be first in your life. This chapter is not written to beg anybody but to inform people to get it right, make God their first priority, not with lip service or ungodly ways but with their hearts, minds, and souls.

If you do not have God first in your life, this means you have allowed other unimportant things to take God's place in your life, and this means

1. you truly don't understand the control or authority God has over your life,

2. you truly do not understand God's grace and mercy, or
3. you are truly caught up in the worldly things and ways.

Perhaps you or others you may know are consumed by worrying over the necessities of life. Consequently, you pursue these things but never develop or place trust in God to provide. I want to encourage you to make time for God and put him first! Do not be too busy working long hours, overtime, or second and third jobs in pursuit of things not important in comparison to the Lord; God is most important.

The Psalmist wrote in Psalm 27:4 (AKJV): *"One thing have I desired of the Lord, that will I seek after; that I may dwell in the house of the Lord all the days of my life, to behold the beauty of the Lord, and to enquire in his temple."*

We must understand who really matters; we must understand the Lord is our salvation; we must understand the Lord is our strength; and we need to give up the bad things, bad habits, and bad attitudes. Satan wants to trap you, but the Lord will show you the safe way. God will sooner or later put an end to those who are playing games or showing no real commitment to him.

Before I close this chapter, I want to share at least three important eternal values with you. Three eternal values every believer in Jesus Christ must have and live; three eternal values every believer must do with the right attitude. I believe it is important to share with you these three eternal values that we must always work on. I have an obligation to advise or inform you to spend your time and resources on these things (three eternal values):

1. Your soul.
2. Develop your relationship with God.
3. Your service to God.

I will briefly expound on the three eternal values because the things of this world will only be here for a little while, but God's kingdom will last forever (1 John 2:17).

First: your soul

Jesus asks, *"What good will it be for a man if he gains the whole world, yet forfeits his soul? Or what can a man give in exchange for his soul?"*

So how much do you think a soul is worth? A million dollars? A billion? How about a trillion? Nobody can really put a price on a soul, and yet so many destroy it by "selling" it to worthless sin and unholy obsessions. Our soul will someday go to one of two places: heaven or hell. If you think your soul is worth more than all the money in the world, then I strongly suggest you look into what Jesus did on the cross.

Second: your relationship with God

Your relationship with God through Jesus Christ, his Son, is another thing that nobody can put a price on. It will not "burn" like the wood, hay, and stubble. Treat your relationship with God like your life depends upon it because it does! So please do not play foolish games with God and his Word! Start living with eternal values! Playing games with God is a serious matter, and the offender or wrongdoer will pay serious consequences—trust God and his promises.

Third: eternal value; your service to God

Nobody can put a price on what you do for God; only he can. He promises to reward those things that are done for him here on earth.

Our heart for God must be real, not fake or phony. I pray that you received the truth. Jesus rejected man-made traditions. God, his Word, and I love people too; don't let the devil confuse you. I am speaking about being confused on who you should follow. Keep your eyes open and ask God for wisdom to understand his plan for your life.

In closing, to seek the kingdom of God and his righteousness means to desire God's righteous rule on this earth. If you are not living with eternal values after reading this chapter, it is time to make a change. I want you to get a sheet or a piece of paper and please write at the top of the paper *"Things I Can Do to Please God."* Write down ten things you can do to please God. It can range from simple things like: "talking with God every day, helping the pastor to win lost souls, make God first priority in my life, become totally committed and obedient to God's Word, step up in ministry, or simply witnessing to my neighbours."

God does not overlook the slightest service to him (Mark 9:41), but you must do it with the right attitude. Golden opportunities to serve God will turn into piles of ash if not done with the right heart before God. Some people talk a lot but show slight or very slim interest in God. God keeps it real in his Word and in his biblical examples.

People who show no real commitment show brighter than they can imagine. Conversely, if we are really committed to God, it will show even brighter. True (genuine or real) Christians, who are committed to Christ, can readily be recognized by what they do. Most times, fake Christians show no real commitment to any particular local church; they just bounce around and around, from church to church, because of their personal or selfish desires. However, I must say though, some people bounce around until they find a Bibleteaching church and a home with less confusion and chaos. But we must remember, God is not the author of confusion or chaos; the devil and us human beings are. Serve God with a right attitude!

NOTES:

Chapter 15

THE GOOD OLD DAYS!

Better is the end of a thing than the beginning thereof: and the patient in spirit is better than the proud in spirit. Be not hasty in thy spirit to be angry: for anger resteth in the bosom of fools. Say not thou, What is the cause that the former days were better than these? for thou dost not enquire wisely concerning this. Wisdom is good with an inheritance: and by it there is profit to them that see the sun.

For wisdom is a defence, and money is a defence: but the excellency of knowledge is that wisdom giveth life to them that have it. Consider the work of God: for who can make that straight, which he hath made crooked? In the day of prosperity be joyful, but in the day of adversity consider: God also hath set the one over against the other, to the end that man should find nothing after him. (Ecclesiastes 7:8–14 AKJV)

Many of us can relate to the "good old days" and know that some things in our past can be very enticing or tempting. The temptation to glorify the past at the expense of the present must be resisted. Why? Because the pleasures or advantages of those good old days may be more imaginary than real. It has been said that the good old days are often a combination or conjunction of "a bad memory" and a "good imagination." Our past is a memory that should minister to us and should persuade or influence us not to be controlled by our past.

People who have been born again through faith in Jesus Christ must not allow or permit the old life to control them. You and many other readers will probably think, *Why not?* Because born-again people's past have been buried, and they are new creatures in Christ. Besides, life is too short to waste on godless or foolish living, especially when you sincerely realize that one day, all will stand before God! My divine assignment here is not to condemn or criticize anybody but to let people know we must be serious about our present. No matter how difficult life may be, there is a job to do, and we must be consistently faithful to God.

This is not about feelings, unpredictable actions, or opinions of others but a time to be serious; a time to pray, a time to show love to the saints, and a time to use your gifts and talents to serve others. The Lord, who gave us the ability, will also give us the strength to do our job faithfully for his glory. I write this final chapter in my book to encourage preparation for the future (in other words, be prepared!) because trials will come. Trials will come to our church, to our homes, to our families, to our marriages, to our jobs, through our children, and even personal persecution or mistreatment by others.

Everybody needs to know that God wants us to use our trials as opportunities to witness for him. The people who wrong us do not know they are really doing us a favor and blessing us with the opportunity to glorify God. Seek to glorify God! Are you prepared?

The Bible has great examples of the good old days! Job is a prime example of the good old days. Job and the problem of suffering is one of the best examples of undeserved suffering recorded in the book of Job. In a matter of minutes, Job, a highly wealthy and godly man, lost all of his material possessions, all of his children, and his health.

His wife gave him no support; she suggested that Job end his misery by cursing God. Then adding anguish upon anguish, Job's friends condemned him rather than consoled or comforted him. To make things even worst or more awful, God seemed to have ignored Job by refusing, for a long time, to answer him and rise to his cause.

Job's intense suffering was financial, emotional, physical, and spiritual. Everyone was against him, and it seemed God was included; a God whom he had served faithfully! Yet Job was a spiritually and morally upright man. Could any suffering be more underserved? Should not such a righteous person be blessed by God? I share this to say, when life is difficult, it is natural or normal for us to look back to the good old days and want to turn back the clock or the hands of time.

Well, that approach is selfish and only adds to your pain.

The example of Job is in chapters 29–30; you can see how many times Job says "I" and "my!" A selfish approach will cause one to make enjoying happiness more important than experiencing holiness. Job listed some of the blessings he had enjoyed and some that prepared him to face his trials with confidence.

So are you using today to grow in the Lord so that you are prepared for tomorrow? Don't fool yourself! Is your life an investment or just enjoyment? Lamenting or mourning the present, Job launched into his complaint about his sufferings. His friends mocked him, and his hope has fled from him.

Job could not return to the past. We cannot return to the past.

So endure the present; face the future; the end will be better than your past. Whenever your circumstances lead you to join Job in the "dust and ashes," remember that the Lord Jesus Christ once was there.

Jesus knows how we feel; he is adequate for our yesterdays, tomorrows as well as our todays. Do not just remember your past enjoyments; also remember God's past mercies, and trust him for the future.

I shared the book Ecclesiastes 7:8–14 (AKJV) in the opening of this chapter: first of all, the book of Ecclesiastes is one of the most misunderstood books of the Bible. Christians have tended either to ignore the message of the book of Ecclesiastes or to regard it as the testimony of a man living apart from God. This is unfortunate, for the book asks relevant, searching questions about the meaning of life, and it declares total futility or uselessness of an existence without God. Like all Scripture, the book of Ecclesiastes benefits and edifies God's people.

The end of a thing is better than its beginning; the patient in spirit is better than the proud in spirit. Solomon observes that even in a world of vanity or pride, wisdom can help us know how to live right. He points out that a goal accomplished is better than setting the goal. When we embark on a goal, a task, or project, we are full of hope, full of expectation, or full of promises. And sometimes, we can be a little full of pride as well! The arrogance of goals is that we declare what will happen. This is not entirely bad but can be a necessary side effect of setting objectives. However, when we reach our goal, and we look back, we see all the obstacles and all the challenges: we see all the missteps and failures along the way and see how God, time and time again, had to come through.

Looking back, we see God's hand in it and how big his part truly was. Being patient in spirit, not giving up, clinging to God gets us to the end of a matter, where pride melts in the face of God's involvement. So, in the setting of the goal, there can be some pride in our spirit. But how much better is the end of the matter, where our patience has helped us see God as the true accomplisher of our purpose?

Do not hasten (rush or hurry) in your spirit to be angry, for anger rests in the bosom of fools. Anger is a normal, often understandable human emotion; yet it is not an attitude that is always pleasing to God. We must learn to control our temper because God's Word tells us that anger labels us as a fool. God's Word also tells us in Proverbs 15:1, "A soft word turns away wrath [anger], but a harsh word stirs up anger."

Do not say, *"Why were the former days better than these?"* For you do not inquire wisely concerning this. This can help relieve the sting or hurt of regrets. Another year has become a part of history. Perhaps you are mindful or aware of opportunities that you have missed or mistakes that you have made. We are so tempted to say, "Oh! If I could have just lived that over again." So many people say, "My, how time flies! I wish I had this year over! I would love to FIX this or that." Do we really want to do it over? Would we really do things differently? It is not wise to wish to go back in time! So don't long for THE GOOD OLD DAYS! This is not wise. The TEMPTATION to glorify the past at the expense of the present must be resisted. As I said earlier in this chapter, the pleasures or advantages of those days may be more imaginary than real.

Wisdom is good with an inheritance and profitable to those who see the sun. Wisdom, like an inheritance, is a GOOD THING and benefits those who see the sun. When wisdom and riches meet IN ONE MAN, it is a happy conjunction or combination; wisdom joined with riches also brings great benefits NOT ONLY to a man's self but to many others in this world. Wisdom is even better when you have money. Both benefit as you go through life. For those who find wisdom, find life.

The Bible says, *"For wisdom is a defense as money is a defense, but the excellence of knowledge is that wisdom gives life to those who have it."*

This tells us that wisdom is protection just as money is protection, but the advantage of knowledge is that wisdom preserves the lives of its possessors or owners. The bottom line: wisdom and money can get you almost anything, but only wisdom can save your life. Money may provide for our natural needs, but money cannot get us into heaven. Money is also no assurance of peace and joy in this world. It is only when you seek after the supernatural knowledge of God that you will achieve the excellency of knowledge that is needed to address all the issues and drama of life. Yes, money is a defense, but the excellency of knowledge is wisdom gives life to them that have it. I am sure you can testify that some people simply don't have the wisdom conveyed.

"Consider the work of God; For who can make straight what He has made crooked?"

Our God is sovereign (he is supreme ruler); he is in the heavens, and he does all that he pleases. We should consider the great things which God has done for us in our lives and our families. We are to accept the way God does things, for who can straighten what he has made crooked?

The crooked that needs straightening out is the presence of afflictions and adversities in life. Both prosperity and adversity come from the hand of God; for prosperity gives thanks, but adversity reflects on the goodness and fullness of the plan of God. In Christ Jesus, we have obtained an inheritance; we have been predestined or predetermined according to the purpose of God who works. ALL THINGS are according to the counsel of his will so that we, who were the first to hope in Christ, might be to the praise of his glory.

"In the day of prosperity, be joyful, but in the day of adversity consider: surely God has appointed the one as well as the other so that man can find out nothing that will come after him" (Ecclesiastes 7:14 KJV).

Every day presented to us is another opportunity to receive or reject what God has in store for us. We can't imagine God would want us to go through adverse or unpleasant times, but we are ready to receive what we perceive to be the blessings of God. God is the same God who blesses and humbles; by his Word, we can see and know that both come from the same loving heart. Celebrating the prosperity of God prepares us to celebrate the promise of his never- ending care and provision. When adversity comes, and it will come, we are then reminded of who our God is—the same yesterday, today, and forever!

You and others may have thoughts of the BIG "Why?" Why has this come upon me? Why did this happen at this time? Why did God allow this? Well, enjoy prosperity while you can, but when hard times strike, realize that both come from God. Remember that nothing is certain in this life! If we do not as humans come to know God and his plan, we will not be able to discern ANYTHING about life or about what will happen after we are gone.

It's important to understand, knowing God is to know that all the answers are ALREADY in him. They are already completed, and they are already done. For us, the challenge is to see them done. We can never know what the future holds, except in him and through him; he alone is complete and finished. His children tomorrow hold his promises and provision through his presence. We must consider the work of God and consider our ways by coming to our senses.

In closing of this chapter, God wants us to consider our ways. In other words, we need to THINK! God wants us to know; he gives both prosperity and adversity, and he knows how much and how long. So instead of peering or looking into the future, now, we need to be prepared for the future, but live in the present and learn to profit from both pain and pleasure (Philippians 4:10–13).

Don't try playing it safe to get the best of both worlds like many are doing. Don't claim to be righteous and wise because we are still on the way and have not arrived yet. That is why God balances our lives with trials and triumphs to keep us from getting proud and setting our ways. It is important for all of us to understand; the better life involves some "bitter things," such as sorrow and rebuke, but the bitter things can make life better.

NOTES:

Chapter 16

MY REAL SOUL MATE

I reserved this final chapter to write about my real true love; my lovely wife, Estell Watson, who consistently, genuinely, and unconditionally loves and supports me. She is my true spiritual soul mate who helped me complete myself and God's will for my life. She must have been named by God as my spiritual half or perfect match and soul mate before I was born. My soul mate's birthday is even on the same day as my mother's.

Proverbs 18:22 (KJV) says, *"Whoso findeth a wife findeth a good thing, and obtaineth favour of the Lord."*

I can truthfully say that I believe God sent this beautiful woman, my wife, Estell, to me. She is a real godly woman, and she sincerely appreciates me, but most importantly, she is a God-fearing woman. She loves and respects God! This is why finding my lovely wife was and still is a good thing. Furthermore, she is beneficial in making me happy, glad, joyful, and appreciated. This woman came from God to me as a REAL blessing and favor.

When God gives you a wife, she is absolutely a good thing! I am so grateful and give God all the glory and all the praise! God knew my situation, and he knew that I needed to open my eyes to see this beautiful woman from him to me. She is a glorious blessing. I truly believe some things are sincerely better when we just let go and let God handle things or situations in our lives, especially when it pertains to getting married and living a godly lifestyle.

I know that God sent me a good woman, but I must say, she did not come without me constantly praying to God for help and her. I prayed to God for a godly woman; I found myself in a situation needing desperate help and asking God to please send me a genuine God-fearing woman. I even believed I said, "Lord, I am tired. Help me find a wife that I know is from you." The Lord's timing was perfect, but I had to trust and wait on the Lord a long, long time. The Lord opened my eyes and granted me wisdom to see the right woman for me and his plan for my life.

Sometimes, I was kind of blurred about the woman God gave me but prayed for clarity and understanding. I did not see the big picture at the moment, but God knows our future and what's best for our lives. Trust God for true love, not yourself or others.

Many strive to define true love with so many different definitions or opinions; true love is really hard to find or define, but it's the kind of love many of us desire and pursue after; sometimes it takes a very, very long time to find true love. My wife and I were honestly true friends nearly three years; we never considered or envisioned ourselves in a passionate or loving relationship, especially in marriage. But unexpected occurrence creeped or sneaked into our personal lives that produced several disappointments, temporary setbacks, struggles, and then an onset of romantic feelings toward each other.

This made things very confusing and shocking at times. We started worrying and communicating about our disturbing feelings of falling in love but also very concerned about our true friendship, our children, and others. We both started feeling undescribed attraction for one another but also remembered or recalled how we became true friends; we did not want to destroy our valued true friendship. We both thought about the several things over and over; we thought about things or people we would have to literally give up in our inner circle. We constantly prayed one-on-one with God and cooperatively with God and believe, together, we followed God's guidance and lead.

Keeping it real, I must truthfully say it was still a struggle initially for both of us because of our friendship and now our feelings toward a romantic or loving relationship. As we deeply considered our feelings and the future, we both constantly prayed individually and collectively, asking and consulting with God for clear guidance and direction. We both inspired each other and did not bring each other down. Even though we both struggled at times with our feelings, friends, families, and others' opinions or their undesirable attitudes, we believed we were each other's soul mate, and we could share our life together.

It is definitely not easy to find the right person in your life. But we realized, together, we were not going to lose hope or be overly concerned about others' undesirable opinions or unwanted personal thoughts. After consistent praying and asking God for guidance and receiving his approval and confirmation, it was a done deal. We decided collectively to move on in our lives together in oneness (marriage) and serve God wholeheartedly every day.

God knew the beautiful woman I needed to love me but most of all love him above all else. We both know God's will in our marriage that passes many understandings. We both identified and recognized the signs God wanted us to be together in a godly relationship. Our trust in God has given us all we need and enjoyment in serving him.

Many years ago, before my wife, Estell, I thought I knew exactly what I needed in living an abundant life that God had planned for me, but I was definitely wrong. One thing I definitely knew this time, everyone wouldn't love or accept me, but God, my wife, my children, and grandchildren would; furthermore, genuine believers in Christ Jesus who really live godly lives and have a genuine spiritual connection with God.

I kept on praying to God for a clear sign to marry or not marry my wife because at the time, so many things were going on or happening in my mind and in my personal life. I could not focus at times or understand my own behavior. One thing for sure, I did know God was with me, and he would give me clear guidance and signs on whether or not my wife, Estell, was the woman for me.

When I did hear from God, it was like he said, "Pay close attention to my words." I was sure it was God because the devil certainly does not want me to confess, repent, or serve God. I also knew the devil will send people in our lives to deceive or throw us offtrack. I believe God also tested me several times, and I failed him and others miserably, but he still did not leave or forsake me. He made it very clear that my wife, Estell, is the woman for me and his plan and will for my life. God always knew the perfect woman for me and the perfect timing. God knew I had lost a lot and needed to trust him; he is in total control of everything.

God knows better than anyone what and who we need in our lives. Since he knows better than we do, why not let God do it? What God does may not be popular for everyone in our lives, but he is God; his opinion definitely counts. I sometimes found myself lost and confused before getting married to Estell but never intended to hurt or disappoint anyone. If you are reading this chapter and have been personally wronged or hurt by me, I am truly sorry. I ask that you please forgive me; it was never my intent to hurt or disappoint anyone. The Bible is very clear on the subject of forgiveness; it's important for our strength and health. God is forgiving; I hope that you are forgiving as well. It's important to forgive those who wronged us; yes, I realize that forgiving is very hard to accept for many, especially when someone deliberately hurts you. Please understand that I personally never meant to wrong or hurt anyone. I never consciously tried to hurt anyone. If I hurt you or anyone, I'm truly sorry.

NOTES:

AN AFTERWORD

This book is not intended to condemn or humiliate anyone; it's basically meant to encouraged professed Christians to be real with God, and be successful in encouraging unbelievers to become believers in Christ Jesus. Furthermore, to help genuine believers show their real faith isn't just for show. We as believers, must be genuine in front of God and others. God knows everything about all of us. The Bible is full of warnings about hypocrites or pretenders. This book will help readers, hearers and doers of God's Word (Bible) notice or become aware of people acting fake. Matthew 7:15-16, states, *"Watch out for false prophets. They come to you in sheep's clothing, but inwardly they are ferocious wolves. By their fruit you will recognize them."*

Jesus forewarns us about false prophets; he says to watch out for them because they appear good outside but are not true inside. We cannot assume people are good because they act or look good on the outside; but the fruit they bear, will eventually disclose their trueness. Leaders of God's people must stay true and practice what they preach. We must not pretend to be leaders and followers of Christ; we must be real leaders and followers! It's like wearing a mask and hiding our true selves but God can see very clearly through and behind the mask. Yes, I know everyone saying they are following Jesus Christ does not have a sincere heart or totally committed to him. But it's important for genuine followers to know who are real, and who not real. But we all must also know Matthew 7:21, tells us, *"not everyone who says "Lord, Lord" will enter the kingdom."*

This book, "Got to Be Real: There is No Faking it With God" is about true actions, not just words. Many will miss their salvation by faking their faith. I am on this divine journey to keep it real, win as many souls as possible for the Lord to save, and forewarn many about pretenders. Lying is a common form of deception; stating something known to be untrue with the intent to deceive. God cannot lie, and the followers of Christ should not lie.

ABOUT THE AUTHOR

Hello, I am Pastor Wilbert L. Watson. Thank you for viewing my author page, and I'd love to have your review of my book. I am a native of Chesterfield, South Carolina. I graduated from Chesterfield High School, the home of the Mighty Golden Rams, class of 1975. I have served in ministry for over twenty years in various teaching, counseling, leadership, and pastoral positions.

I presently serve as the senior pastor of Divine Faith Ministry Church in Petersburg, Virginia. I served twenty-nine years in the United States Army. God is first priority in my life, and I love teaching, preaching, and spreading the Gospel throughout the world. I also love winning souls and leading people to Jesus Christ, our Lord and Savior. I desire to encourage as many people as possible, worldwide, to have a real personal relationship with God.

I am married and love my family, adult children, and grandchildren. I love and care about people and their final eternal destination when leaving this place called earth.

www.ingramcontent.com/pod-product-compliance
Lightning Source LLC
LaVergne TN
LVHW091535070526
838199LV00001B/77